The Art of Resilience

~ Unlocking Sun Tzu's Wisdom for Modern Challenges ~

By

Kenneth So

Foreword

Sun Tzu's teaching harbours invaluable insights beyond its ancient Chinese roots. However, a mere translation from the original text into English would hardly do it justice. Lionel Giles, a renowned British sinologist, committed his expertise to this task in 1910, rendering the entire text of "The Art of War" into English. There needs to be more sense in duplicating these efforts! Even so, it is equally futile to read and study this timeless masterpiece, penned over 2,500 years ago, without understanding how to transpose its teachings into the context of contemporary life and work.

Kenneth So, a retired writer/publisher from Hong Kong who is my regular bridge partner, casually mentioned that he wanted to translate Sun Tzu's "The Art of War" into English. I advised him not to do that, but on the other hand, I encouraged him to try to illuminate and illustrate Sun Tzu's teaching in today's applications! Hence, the idea of "The Art of Resilience" was conceived.

"The Art of Resilience" is intended to be a practical guide to explain the relevance and application of Sun Tzu's teaching in today's activities. This Classic Chinese masterpiece consists of only 6,000 Chinese characters, and its wisdom and education are still relevant and applicable today!

This book aims to contextualise Sun Tzu's teaching and strategies for a diverse audience - from the young to the old, from men to women, and individuals from all walks of life. Its core focus is on the enduring relevance of Sun Tzu's pragmatic wisdom in today's world.

While Sun Tzu's teaching is a military work discussing tactics, it is also often regarded as an invaluable guide to today's various facets of day-to-day lives. It is used as instructional material at the US Military Academy at West Point and recommended reading for Officer cadets at the Royal Military Academy, Sandhurst. Famous business leaders like Bill Gates, Warren Buffet and Masayoshi Son have admitted that their favourite book is "The Art of War". The reason is simple: as the saying goes, business is like a battlefield. Even if one does not engage in business, "The Art of War" can still be applied to interpersonal relationships. In essence, warfare is about the relationship between people. People don't fight boulders or windmills; when it comes to war, it's about fighting other people. Therefore, this is a book that teaches people how to wage war and teaches people how to resolve interpersonal conflicts.

"The Art of Resilience" follows the same order as Sun Tzu's ancient texts and organises the discussion according to the original themes and sequences in thirteen chapters.

Speaking from over four decades of experience as a senior form Maths teacher and a regular Bridge player in several local Bridge Clubs, I've faced a multitude of challenges in areas such as personal management, organisational matters, anger management, the use of logic, the ability to visualise concealed cards, and the execution of strategy. Yet, time and again, I've managed to surmount these hurdles and transform the course of events with Sun Tzu's teachings. It's no hyperbole to assert that this ancient text provides all the necessary wisdom for dealing with my workplace or Bridge game complexities.

In tumultuous times marked by uncertainty, there is no straightforward recipe for success such as "Do this, and you'll triumph". Therefore, let's assimilate and apply Sun Tzu's teachings to endure the thrive without succumbing to defeat!

Albine Patterson
15 June 2023

Preface

At the heart of Sun Tzu's teachings, I find a profound yet often overlooked sentiment: the art of avoiding war rather than engaging in it. The battlefield offers two stark options - victory or defeat, the latter a synonym for death. It is not the count of enemies vanquished that matters, for they are infinite. Instead, it is preserving the one life we each possess and safeguarding what we cherish. Sun Tzu thus posits the most significant achievement as remaining undefeated across a hundred encounters, not necessarily in a hundred battles.

My journey begins with the well-known translation of Sun Tzu's "The Art of War" by Lionel Giles, the esteemed British sinologist whose illustrious career included assistant curator at the British Museum and Keeper of the Department of Oriental Manuscripts and Printed Books. However, I endeavour to reanimate Sun Tzu's central doctrine of peace and avoidance of war in my book, breathing new life into it through enriching examples and engaging illustrations.

"The Art of Resilience" presents a modern-day analysis of Sun Tzu's teachings, rendering them applicable to our contemporary world. I offer this wisdom, once reserved for ancient Chinese monarchs, to everyone, encouraging our readers to delve into the depths of these teachings. I aim to make Sun Tzu's guiding principles widely accessible, helping everyone understand and apply them practically.

The Art of Resilience

I expect that readers, irrespective of their military strategy, business management, or ancient Chinese philosophy background, will find a refreshing and enlightening take on Sun Tzu's teachings. "The Art of Resilience" promotes strategic thinking in pursuing unyielding resilience. It aims to serve as a valuable guide for managers, decision-makers, and individuals from every walk of life who seek to harness Sun Tzu's wisdom to enhance their personal and professional journeys.

I invite you to accompany me on this enlightening exploration of Sun Tzu's central theme of peace and avoidance of warfare. Together, let's strive for global harmony and alleviate the distress caused by unnecessary conflicts.

The indelible mark Sun Tzu's teachings have left on my life is impossible to deny. His principles have navigated me through career transitions, guided risk-taking decisions, informed strategic planning, and facilitated adaptation to changing circumstances and opportunities. Sun Tzu's philosophy is a wellspring of wisdom that can benefit individuals across various disciplines, professions, and life situations.

Writing "The Art of Resilience" has granted me a golden opportunity to share ancient Chinese wisdom and reflect on my journey, my decisions, and how Sun Tzu's principles have shaped my life. His teachings have guided me to look back at the past, deal with the present, and embrace the future with open arms. It gives me immense pleasure to say, "Life is a journey, and my guide is Sun Tzu!"

The Art of Resilience

Embark on this journey with me and unlock Sun Tzu's wisdom for modern challenges!

Kenneth So
15 June 2023

Unlocking Sun Tzu's Wisdom for Modern Challenges

Contents

Chapter I	Initial Planning
Chapter II	Combat
Chapter III	Strategic Attack
Chapter IV	Army Formation
Chapter V	Force Disposition
Chapter VI	Feint and Actuality
Chapter VII	Military Confrontation
Chapter VIII	Nine Changes
Chapter IX	Military March
Chapter X	Topography
Chapter XI	Nine Types of Grounds
Chapter XII	Fire Attack
Chapter XIII	Employing Espionage

Epilogue

Afterword

Chapter I

Initial Planning

> *Sun Tzu said:*
> *Warfare is vital to the state;*
> *it is the ground of life and death,*
> *The path to survival or ruin.*
> *Therefore, measure it in terms of five*
> *fundamental factors,*
> *Compare these with seven elements determining*
> *conditions and seeking their true nature.*
> *The first of these factors is moral influence;*
> *The second is the weather;*
> *The third is terrain;*
> *The fourth is command;*
> *And the fifth is doctrine......*

In the first chapter, Sun Tzu emphasises the critical importance of warfare for a nation's survival and success. He advocates for a comprehensive understanding of military strategy, which he breaks down into five key elements:
1. Moral influence (or moral law)
2. Weather (heaven)
3. Terrain (earth)
4. Command (the general)
5. Doctrine (law or discipline)

These factors are crucial in determining the outcomes of military engagements and require careful study and application.

Sun Tzu's "The Art of War", often considered the preeminent text on military strategy, carries enduring wisdom far beyond its original battlefield context. The "Initial Planning" outlines the importance of comprehensive planning, consideration of various factors, and analysis to forecast outcomes. This chapter explores the practical application of these principles in business strategy, personal development, and public policy, underlining their timeless relevance.

In this Chapter, Sun Tzu stresses the crucial importance of strategic planning to any state, emphasising that military tactics could mean survival or demise, prosperity or downfall. Therefore, understanding the art of war is not just optional; it's an absolute necessity. This art is based on five core factors that should guide any decision-making process when evaluating battlefield conditions.

These factors are Morality, Nature (referred to as Heaven), Terrain (Earth), Leadership (The Commander), and System and order (Method and Discipline).

Morality inspires unity between rulers and their people, compelling them to follow their leader courageously, even in the face of danger. Nature encompasses day and night, cold and heat, and the changing seasons, which can influence a battle's outcome. The terrain includes:
- Aspects like the physical distance.
- Level of danger.
- Security.
- The strategic advantage of different kinds of ground.

The Art of Resilience

Leadership requires the commander to exhibit wisdom, sincerity, benevolence, bravery, and strictness, all traits critical for successful command. System & Order deals with efficiently organising the army, establishing ranks, logistics for supply routes, and controlling military expenditure. Any general should master these five principles. Understanding them leads to victory, while ignorance of them results in defeat.

When assessing military situations, these principles should form the baseline of comparison, considering things like the level of moral unity, the ability of the leaders, the advantage derived from natural and geographical conditions, the level of discipline, the strength of the armies, the quality of training, and the consistency in rewards and punishments. These considerations can be used to predict victory or defeat. A general who follows these principles should be retained, while one who doesn't should be replaced.

Beyond following these principles, a successful leader should also use favourable circumstances. Plans should be flexible and adapted according to changing situations.

Deception plays a central role in warfare; manipulating the enemy's perceptions is critical. When you can attack, appear unable; when active, appear idle; when nearby, seem distant; and vice versa. Deceive the enemy by creating false impressions, luring them into traps, and attacking them where they least expect it. These strategies should remain secret until executed.

We are winning the battle through extensive planning and calculation before the confrontation. Losing happens due to inadequate preparation - the more thoughtful and strategic the planning, the higher the likelihood of victory. A lack of planning will predict defeat. Therefore, one can predict the outcome of a battle based on the depth of planning involved.

Business Strategy: Planning and Analysis

"Initial Planning" underscores the importance of five constant factors: the Moral Law, Heaven, Earth, the Commander, and Method and Discipline. Although initially meant for warfare, these factors can easily translate to a business environment. For example, the Moral Law, which refers to harmony among people, is vital for a successful team. Businesses like Google emphasise creating a healthy, supportive work environment - reflecting Sun Tzu's Moral Law. Their focus on employee satisfaction and teamwork showcases a comprehensive strategy to improve productivity, just as Sun Tzu advocated.

Heaven and Earth, representing physical and temporal conditions, are reminiscent of market dynamics in business. Companies must consider external factors like economic conditions, consumer behaviours, and regulatory changes - analogous to Sun Tzu's Heaven and Earth. For instance, Netflix's shift from DVD rentals to streaming was a strategic response to changing market conditions, much like a military strategist would adapt to the Terrain and weather.

The commander stands for wisdom, sincerity, benevolence, courage, and strictness. In the corporate world, this symbolises effective leadership. For instance, Elon Musk, CEO of SpaceX and Tesla, has shown courage and strictness in his ambitious goals and demanding expectations, embodying Sun Tzu's conception of a leader.

Method and discipline refer to the organisation and control of an army. In business, this resonates with efficient organisation and management. For example, Toyota's lean manufacturing system, which emphasises eliminating waste and improving efficiency, echoes Sun Tzu's emphasis on method and discipline.

Personal Development: Reflective Planning

Sun Tzu's emphasis on planning and self-reflection can significantly benefit personal development. He emphasises understanding oneself and the enemy to ensure victory. In a unique context, "self" refers to individual strengths and weaknesses, while "the enemy" represents challenges or obstacles one faces. One can devise a strategic plan to overcome challenges and achieve personal goals by identifying these factors.

Public Policy: Strategic Planning and Forecasting

Sun Tzu's principles have profound relevance in public policy, where comprehensive planning and forecasting are essential. For example, "Initial Planning" teaches that all warfare is based on deception and that when able to attack, we must seem unable. This principle can apply to negotiations and diplomacy, where a strategic stance and carefully presented image can significantly influence outcomes.

Application of Sun Tzu's "Initial Planning" in the Strategies of Modern Business Titans:

Steve Jobs - the Moral Law: Sun Tzu says the Moral Law signifies unity and harmony among people, a principle that Steve Jobs embedded within Apple. Jobs nurtured a corporate culture encouraging innovation and creativity, seeking to "put a ding in the universe." Despite initial scepticism, his launch of the iPhone demonstrated his faith in his team's harmonious collaboration and innovation, echoing Sun Tzu's concept of Moral Law.

Jack Ma - the Commander: Jack Ma, the founder of Alibaba, embodies Sun Tzu's ideal commander, characterised by wisdom, sincerity, benevolence, courage, and strictness. Ma's visionary leadership and tenacity transformed Alibaba into an e-commerce giant, braving intense competition and sceptical market views. His philosophy, "Customers first, employees second, and shareholders third," resonates with Sun Tzu's idea of a benevolent and wise leader.

Warren Buffett - Heaven, and Earth: Warren Buffett, the 'Oracle of Omaha,' exemplifies Sun Tzu's principles of Heaven and Earth, symbolising physical and temporal conditions, in his investment strategy. Buffett is known for his deep understanding of market conditions and ability to identify undervalued companies. His approach of "buy and hold" and investing in companies with solid fundamentals reflect the strategic consideration of 'Heaven' and 'Earth,' as he navigates the changing terrains of the stock market.

Jeff Bezos - Method and Discipline: Jeff Bezos, the founder of Amazon, clearly applies Method and Discipline. His leadership philosophy of a 'Day 1' mentality, which fosters a start-up's agility and innovation even in a behemoth like Amazon, is a good form of organisational discipline. Additionally, Bezos's commitment to customer satisfaction and continuous improvement parallels Sun Tzu's emphasis on method and discipline. From an online bookstore to a global conglomerate, Amazon's success is a testament to Bezos's strategic planning and disciplined execution.

Conclusion:

Sun Tzu's "Initial Planning" provides a blueprint for strategic planning and decision-making that extends well beyond the battlefield. The principles presented in this chapter hold immense value in contemporary life, offering wisdom for business strategy, personal development, and public policy. Sun Tzu's understanding of human nature, strategy, and planning continues to resonate today, offering guidance for navigating our increasingly complex world. Current business magnates exemplify how Sun Tzu's ancient wisdom remains highly relevant and applicable to today's business world. Through their strategies, they navigate the business landscape and shape it, underlining the enduring relevance of Sun Tzu's "The Art of War."

The statement, "Things you think can't happen can happen at any time - this is life," underscores the uncertainties and unpredictability inherent in life. The first chapter of Sun Tzu's teaching - Initial Planning - emphasises understanding oneself and one's enemy: If you know the enemy and know yourself, you need not fear the result of a hundred battles. If you know yourself but not the enemy, for every victory gained, you will also suffer a defeat. The two notions are related because they speak to the unknown and uncertainty. Sun Tzu's teaching stresses the importance of profoundly understanding oneself and one's opponents for better anticipation and adaptation to potential outcomes. However, as the original statement suggests, certain things we think "can't happen" might indeed occur, pointing to the reality that we can't foresee everything.

In today's business world, these teachings are highly applicable. For instance, companies need to understand their competitors and capabilities to make strategic decisions. However, they also need to realise that market conditions can change abruptly, and scenarios they think "can't happen" might indeed occur - new competitors, technological shifts, or sudden market changes, such as:

Anticipation and Prevention: Understanding the market and competitors allows companies to anticipate and mitigate potential issues, akin to how Sun Tzu advises understanding oneself and the enemy.

Preparation for Unexpected Events: Even if we cannot predict all possible shifts, we should be prepared to react when "impossible" situations occur. This may involve flexible strategies, planning for various scenarios, or maintaining a clear and calm mindset even in challenging situations.

Points to ponder:

1. Life is like a battlefield. Therefore, it's essential to strategise and plan. "Playing it by the ear" is the way of the losers.
2. Things you think can't happen can happen at any time.
3. Plans need to be specific. The more detailed and realistic, the better.
4. The principle of setting plans: Prepare for the worst act optimistically.
5. Remember to consider the challenges of execution.

Chapter II

Combat

> *Sun Tzu said:*
> *In the conduct of war...*
> *A seasoned commander seeks victory in the situation.*
> *He selects and trains his men....*
> *and they exploit the situation.*
> *He does not require perfection.*
> *He makes use of both the prepared and the unprepared.*
> *Such a commander ensures that his men and their resources are well-rested.*
> *Victory should be swift and not prolonged......*

In this chapter, Sun Tzu emphasises the importance of adaptability and resourcefulness in military leadership. He advocates for a commander who can achieve victory through a strategic understanding of the situation rather than relying solely on his troops' brute force or perfect performance. The efficient use of resources and quick achievement of victory are vital principles. Sun Tzu underscores the immense responsibility of military leaders, as their decisions can determine the fate of their people and their country.

Sun Tzu discusses warfare's economic costs and strategic considerations in this chapter. Maintaining a large army is costly, with expenses on supplies, equipment, and other necessities quickly running into thousands of ounces of silver daily (meaning the state treasury will be on the brink of bankruptcy). The drain on resources is more than just financial; a prolonged war can also exhaust your troops' morale and strength. Protracted conflicts can make weapons dull and dampen soldiers' enthusiasm. Laying siege to a town drains your power, and a long campaign can strain a state's resources. When your resources are depleted, other leaders may exploit your weakness. Hence, rushing into war is unwise, but so is an unnecessary delay, as no country benefits from protracted warfare.

The wise leader understands war's destructive nature and strategies to minimise its impact. They don't overtax their people for supplies but instead rely on supplies seized from the enemy, ensuring the army has enough food and decreasing the strain on the state's coffers. Supporting an army from a distance can impoverish the people at home and inflate prices, draining their resources. The cost of repairing or replacing equipment further drains the state's income. Foraging from the enemy is, therefore, crucial. One cartload of enemy provisions equals twenty of your own, easing the burden on your resources. To motivate soldiers to kill the enemy, they must be angry and assured of rewards for their victories. When they capture enemy chariots, they should be rewarded, and the captured equipment should be integrated into your resources. Captured soldiers should be well-treated and used to boost their strength.

The goal in war should be swift victory, not lengthy campaigns. However, a military leader holds the people's fate, as their decisions can lead to peace or endanger the nation. Sun Tzu's teachings in "The Art of War" offer timeless strategic principles that may apply to various situations, including the Russian-Ukrainian conflict. Let's take a close look at how Sun Tzu's fundamental principles might apply:

Understanding the Cost of War: As per Sun Tzu, maintaining an army and combat is expensive, consuming resources not just from the state treasury but also impacting the morale and energy of the people. The conflict between Russia and Ukraine, ongoing intermittently since 2014, has imposed significant economic and social costs on both countries. It has strained their economies, led to the loss of life, displaced people, and destabilised the region.

Avoid Prolonged Warfare: Sun Tzu advises against lengthy conflicts, as they drain resources, weaken resolve, and open vulnerabilities. Given that the war has spanned several years, from Sun Tzu's perspective, this war would indeed lead to the consequences he warned about.

How to Fight the War: If Ukraine were to apply Sun Tzu's teachings, they should consider focusing on strategies that maximise their strengths while exploiting Russia's weaknesses. Sun Tzu emphasises the element of surprise and the importance of knowledge - knowing oneself and the enemy. For Ukraine, this could mean focusing on defensive and guerrilla tactics and leveraging their intimate knowledge of the local terrain. In addition, Sun Tzu's principles suggest Ukraine should seek alliances to strengthen its position, both on the ground and diplomatically.

Securing a Swift Victory: Sun Tzu recommends deception, agility, and adaptability in strategies. Given the current power imbalance, a swift victory might not be plausible in Ukraine. However, a strategic win could be a negotiated peace or a stalemate that secures Ukraine's sovereignty. For that, Ukraine might focus on making the war costly for Russia, diplomatically and economically, to incentivise peace negotiations.

Actionable Steps: Sun Tzu would advise Ukraine to mobilise their population in terms of physical and information warfare to keep morale high and maintain national unity. He also emphasises intelligence gathering to better understand Russia's plans and weak points. Strengthening international alliances and ensuring continued support, economically and militarily, from the international community would also align with Sun Tzu's principles.

These are interpretations based on Sun Tzu's teachings and might only partially encompass the complexities of the actual geopolitical situation, which involves many other factors beyond the scope of this explanation. While initially intended for warfare, Sun Tzu's teachings are full of wisdom that may apply to various aspects of modern life, including business and personal relationships. So, let's break this down:

Business Marketing & Sales:

Understanding the Cost: Just as maintaining an army is expensive, so is acquiring and keeping customers. Successful marketing requires an understanding of the costs involved and managing resources wisely.

Avoid Prolonged Wars: This could mean avoiding long-drawn conflicts with competitors, as it can drain resources and harm the company's reputation. Instead, focus on innovation and providing value to customers.

Securing a Swift Victory: In the business context, an increase in sales could be translated into achieving quick wins in marketing, such as successful product launches or marketing campaigns. However, it's also important to be flexible and adapt marketing strategies as per the market response.

Deception and Surprise: In business, this could translate to outsmarting the competition with unique marketing strategies and surprise product launches.

Management:

Leadership: Just as the commander's virtues are critical in war, so is a leader's integrity in an organisation. Leaders need wisdom, sincerity, benevolence, courage, and strictness to lead their teams effectively.

Understanding and Maximising Resources: Sun Tzu talks about foraging on the enemy, which means leveraging the competitor's weaknesses or market gaps to your advantage.

Organisation and Discipline: The management must organise their teams effectively, establish clear hierarchies, and maintain discipline.

Interpersonal and Intrapersonal Relationships:

Morality: Having moral alignment in personal relationships is critical. It ensures mutual understanding and respect, just like in the context of a ruler and their subjects in Sun Tzu's terms.

Understanding 'The Terrain': Just as understanding the physical terrain is essential in war, understanding the emotional 'terrain' or emotional states of ourselves and others is crucial in maintaining good personal relationships.

Avoiding Prolonged Conflicts: It is healthier to avert lengthy relationship conflicts and strive for a swift resolution.

Using Strengths and Managing Weaknesses: Understanding one's strengths and weaknesses and those of others can significantly improve interpersonal relationships.

In essence, many of the strategic principles in Sun Tzu's teaching - understanding the landscape, knowing when to engage and when to withdraw, leadership, morality, organisation, and discipline - are universally applicable, whether in war, business, or personal relationships. There are two fundamental convictions that a successful entrepreneur will adhere to:

Never part on bad terms - Terminating business relationships on a sour note is possibly the worst strategy an enterprise can adopt. Such an approach may have immediate and long-term repercussions. Immediately, bad breakups are distressing and can negatively affect morale, productivity, and performance. It can create a hostile environment that could hamper business continuity and result in losing trust and cooperation. On a long-term scale, it's essential to understand that industries are often intertwined webs of relationships and reputations, no matter how broad. Poorly handled separations may lead to unfavourable reputations, making forming new alliances or partnerships difficult. The interconnected nature of today's business world means word travels fast; a business with a reputation for ending relationships on bad terms will find it challenging to establish new connections.

There are no perpetual enemies in the business world - Business, unlike personal relationships, is not governed by personal animosities or grudges. Interests and opportunities primarily drive it. It is common in business for yesterday's competitors to become today's partners or for past disagreements to be put aside in the face of mutual benefit. The expression, "There are no perpetual enemies in the business world" encapsulates this fluidity. Despite conflicts, disputes, or competition, business entities may come together for joint ventures, mergers, or partnerships if the situation benefits both parties. It is the pragmatism of business that transcends personal dislikes or past disagreements. Businesses that hold grudges risk taking advantage of potential opportunities. Also, it is essential to remember that individuals change roles and companies. An antagonistic person in one situation could become an ally in another, depending on their new role or company. Keep all communication channels open and respectful.

Conclusion:

Sun Tzu's "Combat" focuses on the pragmatic costs of warfare, the need for strategic planning, resource management, and a goal-oriented approach to conflict. He stresses the importance of not just winning but winning efficiently, underscoring that the real victory lies not in prolonged warfare but in achieving objectives swiftly and with minimal expense. The chapter is a stark reminder that the consequences of war go beyond the battlefield, affecting the economy, society, and the people's morale. It guides handling these realities - from leveraging enemy resources to encouraging proper reward systems and seeking swift victory over long-drawn conflicts.

In business terms, the essence of this chapter is that the focus should always be on achieving outcomes or goals (victory). This is not short-sightedness but efficiency and result-oriented. An overlong project can deplete resources, energy, and morale. In a business context, this underscores a leader's responsibility and power in shaping the company's future. Therefore, any corporate executive must focus on efficiency and achieving clear, tangible goals.

Points to Ponder:

1. Smart strategy: Let the experts work for you. There's no need to face every battle personally.
2. The worst strategy: Both sides part on bad terms.
3. There are no perpetual enemies in the business world.
4. Achieve tangible outcomes or goals rather than entangled in long-term plans or projects.

5. The art of war is not about how many battles you fight but how wisely you deploy your resources to achieve victory.

Chapter III

Strategic Attack

> *Sun Tzu said:*
> *In warfare, the best policy is to preserve the enemy's state intact;*
> *to destroy the enemy's state comes second.*
> *It is better to keep the enemy's army than destroy them.*
> *Preserving the enemy's troops intact is preferable to*
> *decimating the enemy's troops.*
> *Holding the enemy's battalions intact is superior rather than*
> *shattering the enemy's battalions.*
> *Thus, winning a hundred battles is inferior to subduing the enemy without fighting.....*

In this excerpt, Sun Tzu emphasises the importance of strategic preservation and avoiding unnecessary conflict. He places the highest value on strategies that protect the state, the army, and its smaller units rather than those that focus solely on destroying the enemy. Sun Tzu suggests that the most significant military skill lies not in winning battles through confrontation but in achieving victory with minimal conflict and without resorting to war. This approach advocates for strategic intelligence and diplomacy over brute force.

This episode focuses on the mastery of strategic warfare. Sun Tzu begins by advocating the importance of keeping an enemy's country intact rather than destroying it. This strategic approach minimises the loss of resources and lives. Thus, true victory lies in breaking the enemy's resistance without fighting.

Sun Tzu outlines the highest form of leadership, which is to thwart the enemy's plans. Following this, he prioritises preventing the enemy's forces from joining, attacking the enemy in the field, and finally, the least favourable approach, besieging walled cities. He stresses the undesirable outcomes of sieges, such as loss of time, resources, and lives, often with no guaranteed success.

Sun Tzu further emphasises the skills of a leader in subduing the enemy without fighting, capturing cities without siege, and overthrowing kingdoms without lengthy field operations. This stratagem requires assessing the relative strengths of the forces involved and choosing the appropriate approach, whether it's surrounding, attacking, dividing, battling, avoiding, or even fleeing from the enemy.

The General's role is underscored as pivotal, with the state's strength depending on the General's competence. Three key ways a ruler can harm his army are identified as inappropriate commanding, trying to govern the military like a kingdom, and employing officers indiscriminately. Sun Tzu warns that such actions can lead to anarchy and loss of victory.

Five essentials for victory are detailed: knowing when to fight, managing both superior and inferior forces, maintaining a unified spirit throughout the army, being prepared while catching the enemy unprepared, and having military ability without sovereign interference. These five principles act as a guide to predict the outcome of a battle.

Sun Tzu pronounces a famous axiom: knowing both the enemy and oneself leads to victory; knowing only oneself results in alternating victories and defeats; knowing neither guarantees failure. The crux of "Combat" is thus the championing of strategic acumen over brute force, emphasising knowledge, preparation, and exemplary leadership for victory.

In essence, wisdom, tenacity and resilience, as reflected in Sun Tzu's "Combat", is about careful and strategic planning, understanding the landscape, adapting to change, and anticipating challenges to mitigate their impact. Let's delve into concrete examples from different sectors to illustrate how Sun Tzu's "Combat" translates into the "Art of Resilience" in modern life. These examples demonstrate that Sun Tzu's teachings remain relevant in contemporary contexts and can be effectively applied to understand and foster resilience in various fields:

Sales & Marketing:

Apple's Introduction of the iPhone: The iPhone revolutionised the smartphone industry by focusing on user experience over purely technical specifications. Rather than engage in a head-on battle with existing mobile manufacturers, Apple reshaped the market's expectations, subtly undermining its competitors' positions. This can be seen as a form of strategic attack, Apple's release of the iPhone in 2007 subduing the enemy without fighting. Instead of directly competing with other smartphone manufacturers on their terms,

Apple redefined the battlefield by launching a product that combined communication, entertainment, and internet browsing in a single device. Their calculated move reshaped the smartphone market, showing a form of resilience that prevented a head-on battle with competitors.

Amazon's Long-term Strategy: Amazon has consistently pursued a strategy of low-profit margins to win market share - an example of Sun Tzu's principle of the importance of strategic depth and preparedness. By sacrificing short-term profits, Amazon has become the go-to platform for online shopping, effectively changing the terrain of retail marketing.

Human Resources Management:

Zappos's Hiring Strategy: Zappos is known for its unique hiring strategy. The company offers new hires a cash incentive to quit after the initial training period. This strategy allows Zappos to ensure that only committed employees who align with the company's culture remain, which reflects Sun Tzu's principles of strategic selection and taking the initiative.

Southwest Airlines Employee Engagement: Southwest Airlines emphasises a strong company culture and prioritises employee engagement. The company realises that employee satisfaction leads to customer satisfaction, demonstrating Sun Tzu's principle that the morale and condition of the troops are vital to success.

The COVID-19 Pandemic: With the onset of the COVID-19 pandemic, many companies had to transition to remote work rapidly - WFH. Companies that were resilient and succeeded in this transition did so by strategising and calculating the requirements of this "battle." They ensured technological infrastructure was in place, developed new communication protocols, and took measures to maintain employee engagement and morale. This foresight and planning illustrate the resilience concept outlined in Sun Tzu's teachings.

World Politics & International Affairs:

US's Cold War Strategy: The Cold War between the United States and the Soviet Union was characterised by strategic moves and countermoves without direct combat, embodying Sun Tzu's principle of winning without fighting. Through diplomatic, economic, and covert strategies, the US aimed to contain the spread of communism, ultimately contributing to the USSR's dissolution.

China's South China Sea Strategy: China has gradually increased its presence and constructed artificial islands in the South China Sea rather than a more direct, aggressive approach. This gradual approach avoids direct military conflict and aligns with Sun Tzu's teachings in "Strategic Attack".

The Paris Climate Agreement: This international treaty represents a strategic attack designed to subdue the "enemy" of global climate change. Rather than individual countries trying to combat this issue in isolation, nations worldwide have joined forces to develop and implement strategies for reducing greenhouse gas emissions. This collaborative approach illustrates the concept of resilience in the face of a shared global adversary.

EU's GDPR Policy: The European Union's General Data Protection Regulation (GDPR) was a strategic move to safeguard citizens' data and privacy in the digital age. By implementing this policy, the EU has positioned itself as a leader in data protection, influencing global norms and standards. This resilience demonstrates the strategic advantage of shaping the battlefield (in this case, international data privacy norms) instead of reacting to it.

Interpersonal Relationships:

"Conquering the enemy intact": In the context of relationships, this could be interpreted as resolving conflicts without damaging the relationship itself. A good relationship comprises respectful communication, patience, and understanding rather than resorting to harmful words or actions that could "shatter" the connection.

"Thwarting enemy plans": refers to anticipating potential issues or conflicts in a relationship and addressing them proactively. For example, if you know your partner is sensitive about a particular topic, you can carefully navigate discussions around that topic to avoid unnecessary conflict.

"Maintaining a unified spirit throughout": In a relationship, this means maintaining shared goals, values, and mutual respect. For instance, a couple might have a shared vision for their future, or

colleagues might share a common objective in a work project.

The principles in Sun Tzu's "Strategic Attack" also lend themselves to the mastery of perseverance and resilience in various ways. Here's how:

Subduing the Enemy Without Fighting: This principle implies the importance of planning and foresight. By making calculated decisions and strategies, we can prevent unnecessary hardships and bounce back from potential setbacks more quickly. This anticipatory ability is a key component of resilience.

Winning All Battles is Not Supreme Excellence: Supreme Excellence Consists in Breaking the Enemy's Resistance Without Fighting: The essence of this teaching is that the most resilient approach is not necessary to overcome every challenge head-on but to strategise to prevent these challenges from becoming battles in the first place. In this context, resilience means surviving difficulties and navigating situations to avoid or mitigate potential problems.

The General Who Wins a Battle Makes Many Calculations: The idea here is that successful strategy - and therefore resilience - is not based on luck but on careful planning and calculation. A resilient person or organisation anticipates and prepares for potential challenges, enabling a more robust response when adversity strikes.

The Five Factors for Success: These are moral influence, weather (interpreted metaphorically as external conditions), terrain (the competitive landscape), command, and doctrine. The adaptability inherent in considering these five factors reflects resilience. Understanding and adjusting to these factors, you build a strategy that can withstand and adapt to change.

<u>Use of Spies for Every Kind of Business:</u> In a resilience context, this could be interpreted as gathering and using the information to prepare and adjust to change effectively. Knowledge is power in resilience, as it allows for understanding potential risks and developing mitigation strategies.

Conclusion

"Strategic Attack" emphasises the pre-eminence of strategy over confrontation in warfare. Sun Tzu elucidates that the highest form of war is not to fight but to outsmart the enemy, thus avoiding unnecessary losses.

In this context, resilience and tenacity become pillars of strategic foresight. Determination is about maintaining the vision and resolution to see through long-term strategies, not yielding to the temptation of quick victories. It's about enduring the challenges and setbacks during implementation and adhering to the strategic blueprint despite obstacles.

Resilience, conversely, speaks to the ability to adapt swiftly to unforeseen circumstances, mitigating losses and capitalising on opportunities. Sun Tzu's insistence on flexible and adaptable tactics showcases resilience as an integral facet of strategic warfare. It's about bouncing back from tactical disadvantages, adjusting to enemy manoeuvres, and modifying plans when conditions demand it.

Thus, Sun Tzu's third chapter underscores that the art of war is not solely about combat – it's about tenacious and resilient leadership, astute decision-making, and strategic foresight that enables victory without entering the battleground.

Points to Ponder:

1. Strategise to Win: Outwit competitors through superior strategy, not brute force.
2. Understand to Triumph: Know your capabilities and the enemy's vulnerabilities to secure victory.
3. Supreme Excellence: Overcoming challenges without fighting is the ultimate testament to strength.
4. Flexible Planning: Adapt and evolve your strategy to meet changing circumstances.
5. Achieve More with Less: Prioritize efficient use of resources to achieve maximum impact with minimum effort.

Chapter IV

Army Formation

> *Sun Tzu said:*
> *In the past, those skilled in warfare made themselves invincible*
> *and waited for the enemy to be vulnerable.*
> *Being invincible depends on oneself;*
> *the enemy's vulnerability depends on him.*
> *Thus, masters in warfare are those who can secure safety before an offensive attack...*
> *Invincibility lies in the defence, the possibility of victory in the attack.*
> *One skilled in defence hides in the most secret recesses of the earth;*
> *one skilled in attack moves like thunder from the heavens.*
> *Therefore, they are capable of protecting themselves and achieving complete victory.....*

Sun Tzu underscores the strategic importance of defence and offence in warfare in this text. He advises that the key to success in war is first ensuring one's invincibility, which depends on an effective defence. Then, by understanding and exploiting the enemy's vulnerabilities, one can achieve victory. Sun Tzu emphasises that while it is possible to know the principles of winning, the realisation of success depends on various factors, including the actions and responses of the enemy. The imagery of hiding beneath the earth and moving like thunder highlights the contrast between the subtlety and strength required in defence and offence, respectively.

As espoused by Sun Tzu in his acclaimed work "The Art of War", understanding "Army Formation" is vital for leaders and strategists. This chapter emphasises securing one's position to ensure safety before considering offensive manoeuvres. Essentially, this wisdom teaches us that the stability of the leader and his team is paramount to prevent defeat, the prerequisite to launching successful attacks. Good leaders or fighters need to ensure their safety and the safety of their team before considering offensive strategies. Therefore, they put systems and procedures in place to reduce the risk of defeat or failure. Both stability and safety are paramount to preventing loss and the prerequisites to launching successful attacks. However, this does not advocate for a strategy solely reliant on the enemy's mistakes. Akin to gambling at a roulette table, relying on chance instead of deliberate strategic decisions is unsafe. Thus, a skilful leader's role involves crafting a defensive strategy that keeps their team safe while waiting for an opportune moment to strike.

Strategies are classified into two categories: defensive and offensive. Defensive strategies are crucial when you're in a weaker position, while offensive methods should be employed when you have the upper hand. A wise leader discerns when to utilise each of them. For example, protective measures should be favoured at times of vulnerability, safeguarding the team and resources. Conversely, a leader may make bold and offensive moves when opportunities are available and in a position of strength. However, victory is not a mere process of defeating the adversary. It is about doing so with efficiency and efficacy, maintaining an element of subtlety - it's about doing it efficiently and effectively. The best leaders are the ones who win without the whole world knowing about their efforts, making their triumph seem almost effortless. They don't make mistakes, setting themselves up in a position that prevents defeat, and they seize the moment when it's time to defeat the enemy. True strategists know that victory is won before the battle begins - they have done all the necessary preparation and planning, striking only when the conditions are ripe for victory!

A great leader adheres to a moral code and strict discipline, vital elements that augment their ability to influence outcomes. Sun Tzu outlines five critical aspects of military strategy that can be adopted universally:

- Measurement (understanding the landscape and the resources at hand)
- Estimation of quantity (judging the size and strength of forces)
- The calculation (predicting the outcomes of different strategies)
- Balancing of chances (weighing the risks and benefits), and
- Victory (the result of successful planning and execution).

A victorious army has a significant advantage over a defeated one, as a considerable weight does over a small grain. The momentum of a winning force is unstoppable, like a flood breaking through a dam. Sun Tzu's teachings emphasise the importance of thorough preparation, wise decision-making, and efficient execution in leadership and strategy. In this chapter, we learn that:

(1.) *You can't control your opponent:*

You can only control yourself. This strategy finds extensive application in both business and personal spheres. Simply put, you have no power over your competitor's or adversary's actions, decisions, or behaviour, but you have control over how you respond, act, and make decisions. For example, you cannot control a competing firm's marketing strategies, pricing decisions, or innovation process in business. However, you can control how your organisation responds. You can research your competition, understand their tactics, and plan your strategy accordingly. Rather than wasting time and resources attempting to influence uncontrollable factors, you can invest in improving your products, services, or processes.

(2.) *Defence is the best attack:*

The philosophy of "defence is the best attack" is relevant in many fields, including business, sports, and personal development. The idea is to fortify your position so strongly that any attempts to attack or undermine you become futile. Building a solid defence might involve developing a strong brand reputation, securing a robust customer base, or having reliable, high-quality products or services in a business context. These defensive strategies can protect against market volatility, competitor strategies, or shifts in industry trends. For instance, companies prioritising customer satisfaction and loyalty are often better able to withstand competitive pressures. Their solid defensive stance (delighted customers) makes them resilient, and any attempts by competitors to lure customers away can be futile. Similarly, by continuously innovating and staying at the forefront of industry developments, a company can shield itself against the competition - this "defensive" measure effectively becomes offensive.

Both strategies emphasise the importance of self-control and wisdom in concentrating efforts on areas within your control. It's about strengthening your position and responding effectively to outside factors rather than trying to control them directly. **Sun Tzu's** teachings on Tactical Disposition are as applicable today as it was more than two thousand years ago, proving the timelessness and universal application of the principles. Let's look at this teaching in the context of today's business world:

Risk Management:
One practical application of this teaching is risk management. Instead of aggressively pursuing every opportunity for growth, a company prioritises identifying and mitigating potential risks. Doing so may mean improving data security to avoid data breaches, diversifying suppliers to reduce reliance on a single source, or maintaining a solid cash reserve to weather financial storms.

Business Marketing Strategies:
Sun Tzu emphasised the need to fully secure your position before seeking to defeat the enemy. In marketing, this could be interpreted as ensuring that your brand, product, or service is solid, well-defined, and appeals strongly to your target demographic. Therefore, preparation in advance is your defensive strategy. Once you're confident in your offering, you can look for opportunities to outshine your competition

(offensive system) by highlighting your unique selling points or exploiting gaps in the market that your competitors have missed. For example, Apple Inc. first focused on creating innovative, high-quality products that catered to a niche market. Once they established a strong brand and fan base, they launched more aggressive marketing campaigns highlighting their product's superiority over competitors.

Customer Retention:
Another application is customer retention. Instead of solely focusing on acquiring new customers, a company should also focus on not losing existing ones. Retaining customers is often more cost-effective than acquiring new ones, and loyal customers tend to spend more. Strategies include offering excellent customer service, developing a solid loyalty program, or regularly contacting customers to gather feedback and improve products or services. A British retailer, John Lewis, is a good example that excels at customer retention. John Lewis has consistently emphasised customer service, a critical factor in retaining customers. The company also has a robust loyalty program. They are known as the "My John Lewis" membership card. This program provides members with exclusive rewards, offers, and shopping experiences.

Business Management:
In management, ensuring against defeat could mean securing your company's financial position, retaining key staff, maintaining good relationships with suppliers and stakeholders, and staying compliant with industry regulations. Once these elements are in place, you can look for opportunities to expand or innovate. For instance, Amazon secured its position as an online

book retailer before expanding into other product categories and eventually into areas like cloud computing with AWS.

Sustainable Growth:

A business could focus on sustainable growth instead of pursuing aggressive expansion, which might overextend the company's resources and lead to failure. This might involve gradually increasing production capacity, steadily expanding into new markets, or slowly adding new products or services. An excellent example of a company focused on sustainable growth is the Swedish furniture retailer Ikea. It has built a successful global brand through a steady, thoughtful approach to expansion. One key element of Ikea's strategy has been its commitment to sustainability. The company is dedicated to becoming 100% circular and climate positive by 2030 and recycling or reusing all its products and packaging materials.

Human Resources Management:

In HR, you could interpret Sun Tzu's advice as ensuring employees are satisfied, motivated, and productive. Methods or strategies involve everything from fair compensation and benefits to a positive work culture and opportunities for professional development. Then, you can leverage your high-performing workforce to achieve a competitive advantage. For example, Google's HR department focuses heavily on employee satisfaction, providing perks like free meals and flexible work schedules. Once employees are engaged and productive, Google harnesses their creativity and innovation to stay ahead of Competitors.

Interpersonal and Intrapersonal Relationships:

Tactical Disposition might involve self-awareness and self-management (intrapersonal relationships) and understanding and managing relationships with others (interpersonal relationships). In addition, this could include improving your emotional intelligence, communication skills, and conflict-resolution abilities. For example, consider someone who might work on their emotional intelligence and self-confidence before resolving conflicts or negotiating in their personal or professional relationships. Google has been known to encourage employees to work on their emotional intelligence and self-confidence as part of their professional development. Their internal training program, known as "Google's Emotional Intelligence Workshop", is aimed at helping employees improve their understanding of themselves and others, enhancing their teamwork and leadership skills.

Conclusion:

Sun Tzu's teachings on Tactical Dispositions underline the necessity of thorough preparation, wise decision-making, efficient execution, and the understanding and controlling factors leading to success. Regardless of the domain - business, human resources, or personal relationships - strengthening one's position is the key to seizing opportunities effectively and achieving easy victories. Instead of solely focusing on overcoming adversity, emphasise building resilience that helps you withstand future challenges. Remember, you can't control the hardships and trials that life throws at you, but you can undoubtedly control your reactions and attitudes towards them.

A robust resilience strategy includes building strong mental, emotional, and physical defences. These defences, or grit, are your greatest weapons in life's battles. Start by establishing a solid foundation of resilience through nurturing positive traits and effective coping mechanisms. Being resilient means creating conditions for success long before adversity strikes. Prepare for and protect against life's storms, then rise above them: Resilience, in essence, is the art of achieving victory over adversity before it even makes its appearance.

Points to ponder:

1. Don't think about how to win over the opponent; think about how to avoid losing.
2. You can't control your opponent; you can only control yourself.
3. Defence is the best attack.
4. First, create conditions for victory, then engage the enemy. A good warrior will have a chance of winning before stepping onto the battlefield.
5. Prepare and protect, then prevail: Tactical Disposition is the art of winning the battle before it begins.

Chapter V

Force Disposition

> *Sun Tzu said:*
> *In general, employing a large force is the same as using a small one;*
> *it is a matter of division and subdivision.*
> *The way to fight with a large army is the same as the way to fight with a small one;*
> *it is a matter of formation and disposition.*
> *The force that can be brought to bear against the enemy so that he must fight and yet cannot win is a matter of the ordinary and the extraordinary forces.....*

In this chapter, Sun Tzu discusses the principles of managing and employing military forces, regardless of their size. He emphasises that the same principles apply whether commanding a large or small army involves strategic organisation and positioning. Using ordinary (regular) and extraordinary (unexpected) forces in combination to ensure that the enemy is forced into a disadvantageous position is central to his strategy. The analogy of throwing a stone against an egg represents the importance of strategically applying force where the enemy is weakest, emphasising strength against weakness to achieve victory.

Sun Tzu argues that the principles guiding the control of a large force are the same as those conducting a smaller one - it's all about an effective organisation. Whether commanding a massive army or a handful of warriors, the key lies in utilising effective communication, including overt and covert tactics. By managing your forces well, they can stand against the enemy's full force without faltering. Moreover, understanding the strengths and weaknesses of your own and the enemy's forces is like using a grindstone against an egg, a symbol of the power that comes from knowledge and strategy.

Sun Tzu then discusses the methods of combat. Confrontation is often necessary, but one must use indirect methods to achieve victory. When used properly, these tactics are as endless and renewable as the cycles of nature. Just as there are countless melodies from only five musical notes, colours from five primary hues, and tastes from five fundamental flavours, so are the possibilities of manoeuvres from just two forms of attack - direct and indirect. They interplay cyclically, creating an endless array of strategies.

Energy and decision-making are two qualities that Sun Tzu addresses next. He compares the energy of troops to a torrent powerful enough to carry stones and decision-making to a falcon's perfectly timed strike. A good fighter, then, will be formidable in his charge and swift in his decisions.

The text further delves into the potential for seeming chaos within the battlefield. The apparent disorder can be misleading; it does not necessarily mean the actual condition. Instead, it can be a strategy - a show of calculated chaos beneath which lies a highly ordered structure. Similarly, exhibited fear can mask true courage, and apparent weakness can conceal real strength. A clever commander can manipulate the enemy's actions by maintaining deceptive appearances, luring them into a trap.

Lastly, Sun Tzu emphasises the power of combined energy, which doesn't overburden individuals but capitalises on the collective force. By carefully selecting and combining the strengths of his warriors, an intelligent combatant can create a party comparable to a massive stone rolling down a mountain. The energy of such well-coordinated fighters is unstoppable, like a rolling stone that only gains momentum as it descends.

In essence, Sun Tzu centres on the strategic management of forces, the balance between direct and indirect tactics, the importance of deception, and the utilisation of combined energy to create a formidable, unstoppable army.

The principles outlined in Chapter 5 hold timeless wisdom with modern applicability that reaches far beyond ancient battlefields. The fundamentals of strategic control, cyclical tactics, swift decision-making, skilful deception, and the harnessing of collective energy can offer illuminating insights into today's world - particularly in the realm of corporate marketing strategy, a nation's diplomacy and foreign affairs and in the field of product marketing and sales. By applying these principles, we can explore how organisations, governments, and businesses use strategic planning and execution to achieve their objectives, illustrating the enduring relevance of Sun Tzu's wisdom. Let's delve into practical examples to see how these principles are utilised in these modern contexts.

1. *Accumulate strength quietly in ordinary times and strike all at once at critical moments.*

This concept is about preparation and strategic readiness. In today's business world, multinational companies like Amazon and Google invest heavily in R&D, innovation, talent acquisition, and market analysis, even when there is no immediate threat or opportunity. These efforts create a foundation of strength, which can be utilised when critical opportunities or threats arise.

For example, Amazon's massive investment in logistics infrastructure seemed excessive until the COVID-19 pandemic hit. When other companies struggled with supply chains, Amazon was able to leverage its strength and meet the surge in online shopping demand, significantly boosting its market share.

In terms of diplomatic affairs, a country might invest in its military and economic strength or forge strategic alliances in peacetime. Such preparation allows for decisive action during crises, like how NATO allies could swiftly respond to diplomatic or military incidents due to their continuous joint military preparedness exercises.

This concept is highly relevant to sales and marketing. Building a solid brand and cultivating customer loyalty during "ordinary times" can help companies withstand market volatility and competitive pressures. For example, Coca-Cola consistently invests in its brand through marketing and community engagement. When faced with increased competition or market shifts, it can leverage its strong brand identity and customer loyalty to maintain its market position.

2. Acting orderly may be flawless, but flexibility is even better.

This idea emphasises adaptability and resilience. In business, companies must adapt to changing market conditions, technological advancements, or shifts in consumer behaviour. For example, Nokia, once a dominant player in the mobile phone industry, lost its position because it needed to be more flexible to adapt to the smartphone revolution led by Apple and Android.

In diplomacy, conflicts often involve rapidly changing situations, and rigid adherence to initial plans can be disastrous. For instance, during the Cuban Missile Crisis, President Kennedy's ability to adapt to new information and change his strategy led to a peaceful resolution despite the high tension and complexity of the situation.

Marketing campaigns must be flexible to adjust to customer feedback, market trends, or unexpected events. For example, during the COVID-19 pandemic, many companies quickly changed their marketing strategies to reflect the new reality of their customers, shifting focus to online and home-based solutions. Similarly, adjusting one's sales approach based on the customer's feedback and needs is crucial in sales.

3. Accumulate strength in a low-key manner in ordinary times.

This principle suggests building power without drawing unnecessary attention. Tech giants like Apple have mastered this by quietly filing numerous patents for technologies that may not be used for years. Their immense technological strength is often only revealed when they launch revolutionary products.

Countries like China have used this strategy in diplomacy, quietly building economic and diplomatic influence globally over several decades, leading to a significant shift in the global power balance.

In sales and marketing, this could translate into quietly building a robust customer database, researching market trends, and understanding competitor strategies. This can also involve developing a strong product pipeline that keeps future releases secret until the right moment. Apple is a great example, often surprising the market with revolutionary products because they kept their development secret.

4. Everything is about momentum

Momentum refers to the strategic advantage gained when things move in your favour. Companies like Tesla have benefited from its drive, with initial successes in electric vehicles generating investor confidence and public interest, which propelled further growth.

Similarly, nations build momentum in diplomacy by stringing together a series of small victories. The U.S.A. effectively used this strategy during the Cold War. Success in one area (like space exploration with the Apollo missions) provided momentum for initiatives in other fields (political influence, technological supremacy).

In marketing, building momentum can involve stringing together successful campaigns to create brand hype and customer anticipation. For instance, companies like Nike release a series of related advertisements leading up to a major product launch. It builds momentum and creates a significant impact when the product is finally released. In sales, a representative can build momentum by making a series of small deals, which could lead to more significant sales as their confidence and reputation grow.

5. A sense of focus is the driving force that enables continuous progress.

Focus is crucial in achieving any goal. In business, successful companies often have a strong focus on their core competencies and strategic objectives. For instance, Google's motto, "Focus on the user, and all else will follow", reflects how it prioritises user experience, which has driven its success.

In world diplomacy, focus can be seen in countries' long-term strategies. For example, the U.S.'s focus on "freedom and democracy" has guided its foreign policy and international relations for decades, enabling continuous progress in spreading these values globally.

In marketing, a clear, focused message is often more effective than communicating too many things simultaneously. A company that understands its unique value proposition and communicates effectively often outperforms competitors who need a clear focus. Similarly, understanding customer needs and focusing on how your product or service meets those needs can drive success in sales. Amazon's customer-centric approach is an excellent example of a strong focus on progress in both sales and marketing.

Conclusion

Sun Tzu's ancient military wisdom in this chapter can aptly apply to the capacity to bounce back from adversity. Its cultivation parallels the notion of nurturing strength in ordinary times to build our physical, mental, and emotional endurance, preparing ourselves for the uncertainties and challenges of the future.

Similarly, flexibility in handling situations, another core teaching of Sun Tzu, is critical in resilience. No two challenges are the same, so one's ability to adapt to varying circumstances is paramount. A resilient person must navigate adversity as water flows and adjusts according to the landscape.

The principle of quietly accumulating strength echoes the understanding that resilience isn't an instantaneous reaction but a steady build-up of capacities over time. Every small act of courage, every instance of overcoming obstacles, contributes to the more extensive reservoir of resilience.

Sun Tzu says momentum is pivotal in every endeavour and valid for resilience. Momentum provides the thrust needed to overcome difficulties and keep moving forward, even when times are tough.

Lastly, the sense of crisis leading to continuous progress is crucial to resilience. Recognising that problems are inevitable, one learns, grows, and strengthens from each adverse event. Obstacle, in turn, fuels ongoing development and fortifies resilience, resulting in an individual capable of meeting life's challenges with wisdom, strength, and grace.

Points to ponder:

1. Cultivate strength in ordinary times.
2. Victory belongs to those who can handle situations flexibly.
3. Accumulate strength quietly.
4. Everything emphasises "momentum".
5. A sense of crisis leads to continuous progress.

Chapter VI

Feint and Actuality

> *Sun Tzu said:*
> *In warfare, those who arrive first at the battlefield and await the enemy will be at ease, while those who come later and rush into battle will be weary.*
> *Therefore, the skilful warrior brings the enemy to the field of battle and does not*
> *let himself be drawn there by his opponent.*
> *He can induce the enemy to come to him and thus benefits from a favourable position.*
> *He can prevent the enemy from engaging, thereby causing harm to the enemy.*
> *Therefore, if the enemy is at ease, be able to exhaust him; if well fed, starve him;*
> *if resting, make him move.....*

In this chapter, Sun Tzu emphasises the strategic advantage of controlling the circumstances of a battle. He advocates for being proactive and positioning oneself advantageously, forcing the enemy to react under less favourable conditions. This involves manipulating the enemy's movements and decisions, exploiting their weaknesses, and dictating the terms of engagement. The underlying principle is to gain superiority through confrontation, strategic planning, and psychological warfare, conserving one's resources while depleting enemy ones.

Sun Tzu's "The Art of War" offers timeless insights into strategy. He highlights the importance of being the first to act and gaining the upper hand rather than responding in haste and exhaustion. Strategists must impose their will without being influenced by opponents, luring adversaries when advantageous and making themselves unreachable when beneficial. This dynamic is much like a game of chess where one forces their opponent to react to their moves.

Swift, unexpected actions are essential, like launching a surprise product in a market with scarce competition. Defending only unassailable positions and striking undefended areas is critical to ensuring safety and success. The art of warfare lies in the subtlety of the attack, the swiftness of retreat, and the ability to induce the enemy to engage or dissuade them at our convenience.

Understanding the enemy's disposition while keeping our concealed helps concentrate our resources. Sun Tzu suggests acting as a single entity versus a divided opponent, using the sheer advantage of unity against their fragmentation.

Our battle plans should be confidential to keep the enemy guessing, compelling them to dilute their resources in anticipation of multiple attacks. The resulting numerical superiority gives us an advantage. Precise knowledge of the battlefield enables effective coordination and resource deployment. Without it, support mechanisms falter, even when the enemy seems numerically superior.

A clever strategist seeks to discover the opponent's plans, their strengths, and weaknesses. The art of strategy lies in veiling one's plans while manipulating the enemy to reveal theirs. Victory emerges not from repeated tactics but from adapting to an infinite variety of situations.

Lastly, Sun Tzu compares military tactics to water. It avoids strength, hits weakness, and adapts its course based on the landscape. Just like a soldier should strategise considering the opponent's Disposition. Victory belongs to those who adjust their tactics like water, reflective of shifting elements and seasons, recognising that no condition remains constant in warfare.

The teachings from this chapter can be extrapolated into various fields, including sales and marketing, management, interpersonal relationships, and world politics.

Sales and Marketing

Being first in the field: In the marketing realm, this could translate to being first to the market with a new product or service, enabling a business to establish brand recognition and loyalty before competitors enter the space. The classic example is Apple's iPhone, which, although it wasn't the first smartphone, was the first to simplify the smartphone experience, causing rivals to scramble to catch up.

Attacking undefended places: This strategy translates to finding untapped or under-served markets where competition is minimal. For example, Netflix pivoted from DVD rental to streaming services, focusing on an area that was relatively under-served at the time.

Devising stratagems: Companies that strategise and plan their marketing tactics well in advance have the upper hand. Coca-Cola, for example, has used various schemes throughout its history, from its "Share a Coke" campaign to the "Open Happiness" initiative.

Concealing strength: Companies sometimes hide their plans or upcoming products to create a surprise effect and gain an edge over competitors. An example is the secrecy around new Apple product launches, which builds anticipation and excitement.

Man Management

Discovering the enemy's dispositions: In the context of management, this could mean understanding the strengths, weaknesses, and motivations of your team members. Managers who can assign tasks that align with individual strengths and ambitions tend to have more engaged and productive teams.

Concealing dispositions: This applies to managing information flow within an organisation. While transparency is essential, there may be times when revealing too much about a pending decision can lead to speculation and anxiety among the staff. Thus, a good manager knows when to disclose information and when to hold back.

Maintaining morale: Effective managers maintain high team morale even in challenging times. It is analogous to how a general keeps the spirit of his soldiers high in adverse situations. Google, for example, is known for fostering a positive work environment and various employee perks.

Assigning suitable roles: Managers, like generals, should know the capabilities of their team members and give them positions that best suit their abilities. The practice of promoting from within, seen in many successful companies like 3M and GE, is a testament to this concept.

Interpersonal Relationships

Scheme to discover his plans: In interpersonal relationships, this could translate into taking time to understand the needs, wants, and expectations of the other party in the connection. The more you know the person's motivations and goals, the better you can interact with them.

Water-like flexibility: This principle emphasises the importance of flexibility in relationships. Just as water adjusts its path based on the terrain, we should be willing to adapt our behaviour and attitudes based on the changing dynamics of our relationships.

Constant communications: In a relationship, consistent and clear communication helps to prevent misunderstandings and conflicts. Regular check-ins or open conversations about issues in the relationship are examples of this.

Understanding differences: In any relationship, recognising and respecting the other party's differing opinions, backgrounds, and experiences leads to a healthier relationship. The concept of 'agreeing to disagree' is an example of this.

World Politics

Avoiding the strong, attacking the weak: This concept is often seen in international politics. Nations usually avoid confrontations with powerful countries but exert power on more vulnerable nations. For example, larger muscles may exert economic or political influence over smaller nations without directly engaging in conflicts.

Not revealing the spot of battle: In the international political arena, this can be seen in diplomatic negotiations. Countries often keep their strategies and concessions close to their chest until the last minute to maintain a competitive edge in negotiations.

Creating alliances: Countries often form alliances to strengthen their position on the global stage, similar to how armies form alliances in warfare. For example, the formation of NATO during the Cold War was a strategic move to consolidate power against the perceived threat of the then-Soviet Union.

Influence through non-military means: Some countries often wield their influence through economic and cultural means instead of military force. The British Council is the UK's international organisation for cultural relations and education opportunities. It supports peace and prosperity by building connections, understanding and trust between people in the UK and countries worldwide. The Alliance Francaise, for the past 135 years or so, has been offering French language courses, promoting French and French-speaking cultures, and encouraging intercultural dialogue and exchanges worldwide.

Sun Tzu's "Art of War" provides valuable insights and strategies that may be applicable in various areas of life. The central themes of understanding one's and the other's strengths and weaknesses, maintaining strategic flexibility, and the element of surprise are universally applicable across different domains. The two most valuable lessons to take home in the chapter are:

Avoid projects where masters gather. This suggests one should not rush into competitive areas with established, successful entities ("masters"). Instead, it's recommended to focus on your skill development and target a niche where you can truly make a difference and stand out. It would be best if you never competed with the big players, but it might be beneficial to develop unique competencies to help you carve out your own space.

Business Example: Netflix is a good illustration. Initially, they were an online DVD rental service, avoiding direct competition with the brick-and-mortar giant, Blockbuster. This allowed them to focus on their unique strengths: understanding the internet market and logistics for shipping physical media. They moved into streaming services as they grew and developed their skills and competencies.

Innovation Example: Consider the rise of plant-based meats. Rather than trying to compete directly with traditional meat producers, companies like Beyond Meat and Impossible Foods developed a novel product for a growing niche of consumers interested in plant-based diets. As their technologies and recipes improved, they gained more market share, even finding space on supermarket shelves and fast-food restaurant menus alongside traditional meat products.

Unexpected situations are not coincidental, but you have ignored the movement beneath the surface. This implies that "unexpected" occurrences in business often result from underlying trends or patterns that have been overlooked. By paying closer attention to these less obvious factors, one may anticipate and prepare for unexpected situations rather than being caught off guard.

Business Example: **The rise of the digital camera** was a disruptive innovation that decimated the traditional film industry. For companies like Kodak, the advent of digital cameras was an "unexpected situation". However, the trend towards digital was a movement beneath the surface that had been progressing for years. If Kodak had paid closer attention to this underlying shift, they might have been able to pivot their business strategy more effectively and maintain their industry standing.

Innovation Example: **The rapid** shift to remote work during the COVID-19 pandemic may have seemed sudden and unexpected to many companies. However, the trend towards remote and flexible work has been growing for years, accelerated by advancements in communication technologies and changing attitudes towards work-life balance. Companies that recognised and adapted to this underlying movement were better positioned to weather the impacts of the pandemic. They not only survived but also thrived during this period of upheaval.

Conclusion

Sun Tzu's strategies highlight the importance of understanding one's unique strengths and observing underlying trends in business and innovation environments. Recognising the "movement beneath the surface" can help to anticipate and effectively respond to future changes.

Resilience, an art and a science, transcends beyond simply enduring or coping with adversities. It is an active process that allows individuals to navigate life's ebbs and flows, not merely survive them. It's an interplay between understanding your strengths and weaknesses and learning how to leverage them, even under unfavourable circumstances.

Adaptive confrontation is an essential characteristic of resilience; we must recognise our weaknesses and others' strengths, using them as leverage to control situations rather than being controlled. Resilience doesn't mean an endless reservoir of power. It's about discerning when it's most needed and utilising it wisely. The art of resilience shines through in winning without fighting, avoiding conflicts and achieving goals effortlessly.

In summary, resilience is the art of strategic living. It's about understanding oneself, harnessing personal traits, being vigilant to changes, and striving for non-conflictual wins. These factors make resilience a survival strategy and a blueprint for a fulfilled life.

Points to ponder:

1. Hit where they're weak. Control and don't be controlled.
2. Use your best force when it matters most.
3. Avoid crowded expert fields. Build your skills.
4. Surprises often mean missed clues.
5. Use your strengths and weaknesses to win without fighting.

Chapter VII

Military Confrontation

Sun Tzu said:
In the use of troops, when a general receives his commands from the sovereign,
assembles the armies, and musters the masses,
nothing is more complex than military operations.
The difficulty of military operations lies in making the devious route the most direct and misfortune the most beneficial.
Therefore, by taking a circuitous route and enticing the enemy with advantages,
the later arrivals will march swiftly and arrive before those who took the direct way.
This is to know the calculations of the indirect and direct paths.
Thus, deceit achieves success in war, and the army is moved by advantage.
Variations and adaptability are a matter of division and reunion.
Therefore, its rapidity is that of the wind, its silence of the forest, its ravaging like fire,
its immovability like a mountain,
its difficulty to know like the dark,
its movement like thunder.
Plunder the countryside to separate the masses,
spread out over the land to distribute the benefits, and weigh the situation before moving.
The one who knows the art of the indirect and direct path will win.
This is the method of military operations.....

In this chapter, Sun Tzu discusses the complexity and subtleties of military strategy. He emphasises the importance of adaptability, deception, and indirect approaches to gain an advantage over the enemy. Sun Tzu advises that the victorious general must be able to assess and manipulate situations, turning apparent disadvantages into opportunities. He uses vivid metaphors to describe the ideal qualities of an army, such as speed, stealth, strength, and unpredictability.

Sun Tzu's seventh chapter in "The Art of War" is a comprehensive guide to effectively managing resources. Today, it continues to bear profound relevance in the business world. It underlines the fundamental principle of maximising returns while minimising investment. Sun Tzu stresses the importance of efficient logistics and operations, which translates today as lean management and cost-effectiveness. In this light, every business, like an army, has limited resources and faces challenges in market competition, cost constraints, and customer demands. By mastering the balance of deploying these resources intelligently, without overextension or wastage, companies can position themselves for sustained success.

Sun Tzu emphasises the complexity of tactical manoeuvres in war. These manoeuvres involve manipulating your position and the enemy's to gain an advantage, even if it means taking an indirect approach. The art of war also requires harmonising various components of your forces. Operating a disciplined army is beneficial, whereas handling an undisciplined group can lead to catastrophe.

Sun Tzu points out that timing is crucial when moving your troops to seize an advantage. Moving the entire army can be slow and might make you miss the opportunity. On the other hand, sending a smaller force quickly might require leaving behind crucial supplies. If you push your troops to march faster and further than usual to gain an advantage, you might lose a significant portion of your forces due to exhaustion. An army without supplies, a baggage train, or supply bases is doomed. Knowing the terrain and understanding neighbouring states' intentions is essential before making military movements. Local guides can help utilise natural advantages.

Sun Tzu also stresses that deception is vital in warfare. Decisions about concentrating or dividing troops should be based on the situation. Be fast like the wind, dense like a forest, destructive like fire, immovable like a mountain, mysterious like the night, and strike like a thunderbolt. When you seize a territory, distribute the spoils among your soldiers to boost morale. Every action must be considered carefully. Victory goes to those who master the skill of tactical deviation.

Sun Tzu emphasises communication in battle is essential, but spoken words only carry a little, so use gongs, drums, banners, and flags to guide your troops. These tools help focus the army's attention, create unity, and prevent individuals from advancing or retreating independently. Using different signals for day and night combat ensures efficient communication.

Sun Tzu talks about how the mental state of the army and its commander can impact the outcome of a battle. Soldiers are typically most energetic in the morning, less so by noon, and they desire to return to camp by evening. Wise generals avoid attacking when the enemy's morale is high and attack when it is low. The art of war involves:

- Being calm and disciplined.
- Observing the enemy's chaos.
- Preserving one's energy.
- Striking when the enemy is weary and far from their goal.

He advises not to engage an enemy that appears organised and confident. Avoid battling an enemy uphill or meeting them when they are coming downhill. Don't chase an enemy pretending to flee or attack a spirited army. Avoid the enemy's traps. Don't obstruct an army trying to return home. When surrounding an enemy, leave them a way out; a desperate enemy can fight fiercely. These teachings reflect the subtleties of warfare strategy.

I wish to explain Sun Tzu's teachings in "Military Confrontation" with relevance to modern sales and marketing and how the principles can be used in today's business context below:

Strategic and Tactical Planning: Sun Tzu emphasised planning and executing manoeuvres in warfare. Similarly, businesses like Procter & Gamble, renowned for their strategic marketing, carefully plan their strategies based on comprehensive research and competitive analysis. They tactically place their products in the market, often making indirect approaches to outmanoeuvre competition.

Understanding and Using Resources Effectively: Companies must efficiently understand and use their capabilities and resources. With its logistics and supply chain mastery, Amazon ensures products are delivered swiftly to customers, sometimes preceding short-term gains for long-term profitability and market share.

Importance of Market Knowledge and Local Expertise: Understanding the terrain equates to understanding your market in business. Coca-Cola, known for its extensive global presence, adapts its products to suit local tastes, demonstrating how a deep understanding of local markets can drive sales.

Rapid and Decisive Action: Sun Tzu's principle of acting quickly and decisively is evident in the tech industry. Google, for instance, swiftly introduces updates or new features to outpace competitors, making its moves with "the speed of the wind and the strength of a forest."

Rewarding Your Team: Sun Tzu's practice of dividing spoils among soldiers can be applied to employee incentive programs. Companies like Starbucks provide generous employee benefits, acknowledging that rewarding employees boosts morale and Productivity.

Effective Communication: Visual and auditory signals in warfare translate to clear and engaging marketing in business. Nike, known for its iconic "Just Do It" slogan and the swoosh logo, effectively communicates its brand message, guiding and focusing its consumers on its products.

Understanding Customer Behaviour: Sun Tzu's observation on soldiers' moods is akin to understanding customer purchasing habits in business. E-commerce companies like Alibaba use big data analytics to study customer behaviour and time their sales promotions accordingly.

Careful Decision-making: Sun Tzu's cautions against specific engagements in warfare can be compared to business decisions on when to compete or collaborate. Microsoft, for instance, chose to partner with competitors like Red Hat and Oracle in cloud computing, recognising that cooperation in certain areas can be more beneficial than competition.

These examples illustrate the timelessness of Sun Tzu's principles, as they find relevance in warfare and modern sales and marketing. Companies that strategically manoeuvre, communicate effectively and understand their customers and markets will likely succeed in the competitive business landscape.

In this chapter, Sun Tzu provides profound insights into the complexities of warfare, especially around the execution of strategic manoeuvres and managing one's resources. Sun Tzu equates the art of manoeuvring an army to the delicate task of managing a complex, dynamic organisation.

In warfare, these manoeuvres involve carefully coordinated movements, usually deceptive, to disorient the enemy and secure an advantageous position. These can range from taking an intentionally circuitous route to lure the enemy away to acting after the enemy but reaching the objective ahead of them. The underlying principle is not brute force or straight-line speed but the art of indirect approach and subtlety in execution.

Sun Tzu also emphasises the importance of an army's unity and discipline. A coordinated and well-disciplined army can execute complex manoeuvres and yield significant advantages. However, an undisciplined group can quickly devolve into chaos and become a liability.

The timing of movements is a critical factor in warfare. Sun Tzu cautions against rushing to gain an advantage by overextending one's forces. Pushing your army to march faster and further than usual, motivated by the prospect of gaining an advantage, may yield the opposite result, as the strain could leave the army vulnerable and significantly reduced in size. Sun Tzu implies that an army without provisions or a reliable supply chain is vulnerable. Further, the need to understand the terrain and utilise local guides underlines the value of local knowledge in gaining a competitive edge.

Sun Tzu advocates for deception and speed in warfare. Rapid movements, impenetrable plans, and strikes likened to thunderbolts are promoted as a valuable strategy. The concept of rewarding your soldiers with spoils from successful campaigns signifies the importance of morale in ensuring the commitment and effectiveness of your troops.

The chapter underscores the importance of communication within an army. Sun Tzu suggests that verbal communication is insufficient on the battlefield and instead recommends using visual and auditory signals, such as gongs, drums, banners, and flags, to guide and focus the troops. Doing so improves communication and fosters unity among the soldiers, making it difficult for individuals to act independently, whether out of courage or fear.

Sun Tzu further delves into the psychological aspects of warfare, suggesting that the time of day significantly affects a soldier's spirit and, thus, their combat effectiveness. He recommends attacking the enemy when their morale is low, thus turning their state of mind against them.

The chapter concludes with several cautionary pieces of advice. Sun Tzu discourages engaging an enemy that appears organised and confident or attacking uphill or against an enemy moving downhill. He warns against pursuing an enemy pretending to flee, attacking spirited soldiers, falling for enemy traps, interfering with an army trying to return home, or cornering an enemy without providing them with a way to escape.

Sun Tzu's teachings in this chapter are as much about understanding oneself as the enemy. It emphasises careful planning, prudent decision-making, effective communication, understanding the psychology of one's troops, and respecting the enemy's potential responses. While framed in the context of ancient warfare, the principles can apply to any situation where strategy, coordination, and manoeuvring are critical to success.

Conclusion

Sun Tzu's "Military Confrontation" offers valuable insights for cultivating resilience, which remains as relevant today as it was in ancient times. Sun Tzu emphasises the importance of unity and informed decisions in any endeavour. In a resilience context, this means understanding one's environment and adapting to it while leveraging the team's strengths. In essence, informed actions driven by a harmonised team can pave the way for overcoming adversity and achieving success.

The essence of resilience is also reflected in "Strike with Thunder, Stand like a Mountain" - Speed & Steadfastness. Here, Sun Tzu promotes acting swiftly yet staying resolute in facing challenges.

Finally, discerning when to act and hold back is critical in managing crises and adversity. Having the wisdom to make such judgments adds a layer of resilience as it helps avoid unnecessary risks while maximising opportunities. In essence, the teachings of Sun Tzu offer a timeless framework for building strength, emphasising harmony, informed action, steadfastness, communication, unity, and discernment.

Points to ponder:

1. Harmonise to Mobilise – Sync to Success.

2. Know Your Terrain, Utilise Your Guides - Power in Informed Action.
3. Strike with Thunder, Stand like a Mountain - Speed & Steadfastness: The Ultimate Duo.
4. Communicate like a Drum, Unify like a Banner - Your Vision, Their Unity.
5. Wisdom through Discernment - Timing Makes the Difference.

Chapter VIII

Nine Changes

> *Sun Tzu said:*
> *In military deployment, leaders must stay vigilant in nine variable situations,*
> *namely: on impassable terrain, do not encamp;*
> *in intersecting landscape, join forces;*
> *in isolated terrain, do not linger;*
> *in surrounded terrain, devise strategies;*
> *in desperate terrain, charge forward;*
> *there are routes not to be followed;*
> *armies not to be attacked;*
> *towns or positions not to be contested;*
> *and commands not to be obeyed.*
> *Therefore, a general well-versed in the advantages of the "Nine Changes"*
> *understands the art of warfare….*

In this text, Sun Tzu guides how to respond to different types of terrain and situations in warfare. He advises avoiding certain actions in specific circumstances, such as not encamping in impassable terrain or not lingering in isolated areas. The idea is to understand and adapt to the environment and situation.

Moreover, Sun Tzu emphasises the importance of discretion in warfare - understanding when not to act, even in defiance of orders, if it is against the state's best interest. This passage highlights the importance of strategic judgment and adaptability in military leadership, recognising that knowing when and how to respond to changing situations is crucial in warfare.

Chapter VIII of Sun Tzu's "The Art of War", titled "Nine Changes", delves into the dynamic nature of warfare and the need for flexibility in executing plans. He underscores the importance of adapting to the situation at hand, given the unpredictable and ever-changing circumstances on the battlefield.

Sun Tzu begins by acknowledging that while a general receives commands from the sovereign, the execution of the war strategy rests on the general's shoulders. He emphasises that military decisions need to consider the topography and strategic positions on the battlefield. For instance, the general should avoid encamping in rugged terrain, seek alliances at high road intersections, avoid dangerously isolated places, employ stratagems in hemmed-in situations, and be prepared to fight in desperate positions.

He also suggests that certain situations should be consciously avoided, such as not following certain roads, not attacking specific armies, not besieging particular towns, not contesting certain positions, and even not obeying specific commands of the sovereign.

Sun Tzu advises blending considerations of advantages and disadvantages in the planning phase. It's essential to temper expectations of success with a clear understanding of potential pitfalls. We can extricate ourselves from misfortune if we're always ready to seize an advantage amidst difficulties. He recommends causing trouble for hostile chiefs, keeping them engaged, and using allurements to manipulate their movements.

This Chapter reinforces the importance of readiness in warfare. The general should not rely on the enemy's inaction or lack of aggression but should focus on making his position unassailable. The capacity to receive the enemy and the preparation to respond adequately are emphasised over mere hope or wishful thinking.

Sun Tzu concludes his teaching by highlighting five dangerous faults that can afflict a general:
- Recklessness that leads to destruction.
- Cowardice that results in capture.
- A hasty temper that insults can provoke.
- A delicacy of honour that is sensitive to shame.
- Over-solicitude for his men, exposing him to worry and trouble.

He argues that these faults can ruin the conduct of war, and when an army is defeated and its leader killed, the cause can almost always be traced back to these five faults. Sun Tzu urges generals to meditate on these potential flaws, underlining the need for self-awareness and ineffective leadership.

Sun Tzu's "Nine Changes" teaches flexibility, readiness, a clear understanding of the strategic use of advantages and disadvantages, and awareness of potential leadership faults. It illustrates the complexity of warfare and underscores the need for adaptable strategies and mindful leadership.

Sun Tzu provides invaluable insight applicable to current business scenarios, including sales and marketing, human resources management, and international diplomacy. Let's explore these principles in a contemporary context.

Sales & Marketing Strategies:

We can relate the principles in this Chapter to choosing the right markets and competitive strategy. For instance, Tesla understood this well when introducing luxury electric cars, competing in a niche market instead of a mass market that traditional automakers dominated. They didn't attack the "army" (competitors) where they were strongest but chose a path less travelled (electric vehicles) to gain an advantage.

Human Resources Management

A reckless leader might take unnecessary risks, leading to potential business failure. Cowardice might mean avoiding difficult but necessary decisions, while a hasty temper could lead to poor interpersonal relationships. Similarly, being overly sensitive to criticism might prevent a leader from taking constructive feedback, and excessive worry for employees might lead to micromanagement. Satya Nadella, CEO of Microsoft, is an example of a leader who embodies the balance - he transformed the company culture to one of learning, inclusion, and employee empowerment, thus avoiding these pitfalls.

This could be compared to the importance of ongoing employee training and development in human resources. Google, for instance, invests heavily in training its employees, not because they anticipate a specific problem but to ensure that their teams are ready to face any challenge. They've created an 'unassailable' position through a skilled, adaptable workforce.

International Diplomatic Relationship

These principles in this Chapter apply well to the sphere of international diplomacy. Countries, like businesses, need to identify allies and build relationships for mutual benefit. For example, the Paris Climate Agreement symbolises global allies joining to tackle climate change. Similarly, not lingering in dangerously isolated positions can be applied to countries forming alliances like NATO for collective security, ensuring they are not 'isolated' and vulnerable.

These strategies could be seen in the diplomacy between countries during international crises. For instance, during the COVID-19 pandemic, many countries seized the opportunity to strengthen bilateral relationships through vaccine diplomacy. Countries like India and China used their manufacturing capabilities to provide vaccines to other nations, enhancing their diplomatic ties and influence.

Conclusion

Sun Tzu's timeless teachings provide strategic guidance for warfare and offer profound wisdom applicable to the modern business environment, human resources management, and international diplomacy. His emphasis on flexible tactics, strategic alliances, understanding of the competitive landscape, and self-awareness in leadership continue to be relevant in navigating today's multifaceted challenges.

His emphasis on flexible tactics underscores the importance of adaptability and innovation. In the business world, markets are perpetually evolving, consumer preferences constantly shift, and technological advancements are ceaselessly emerging. As such, businesses that adopt flexible strategies, willing to pivot and adapt in response to these changes, are likely to thrive. This approach is equally relevant to international diplomacy, where changing geopolitical landscapes necessitate flexible and adaptive negotiation tactics.

Strategic alliances, another fundamental tenet of Sun Tzu's teachings, emphasise the power of collaboration and partnership. Building partnerships through solid teamwork and collaboration can enhance organisational performance and employee engagement in human resources management in today's globalised business environment. Moreover, in international diplomacy, forming strategic alliances is often pivotal in achieving shared objectives and maintaining global peace and stability.

In essence, while formulated in the context of ancient warfare, Sun Tzu's principles continue to hold immense relevance in navigating the complex challenges of today's world. His insights offer timeless wisdom that can guide strategic planning, leadership, and decision-making across various spheres of modern life.

This Chapter provides critical lessons on the art or mastery of resilience. The strength lies in adapting and evolving in adversity and changing circumstances.

The Art of Resilience

On the battlefield of life, affairs are perpetually shifting, presenting both expected and unexpected challenges. Being resilient is imperative to abandon rigidity and welcome adaptability. Rigidity, or the inability to modify strategies and approaches in response to changing dynamics, can hinder progress and lead to failure. On the other hand, adaptability enables individuals to navigate through changing situations, learn from them, and emerge stronger, demonstrating resilience.

Resilience does not merely denote the ability to withstand adversity; it also entails the skill to identify opportunities amid difficulties. Challenges are inevitable, but a resilient individual perceives them not as setbacks but as stepping stones to growth and development. This positive mindset aids in transforming adversity into an advantage, demonstrating true resilience.

Reliance to the failure of opponents exhibits a reactive mindset. Instead, a resilient person strives to fortify one's position, rendering it impregnable to external shocks. This proactivity translates into enhanced self-reliance, which is a cornerstone of resilience. "Leadership pitfalls can turn a victor into a victim; self-awareness is paramount," underscores the significance of self-awareness in building strength. Understanding and acknowledging personal weaknesses is crucial, as they can jeopardise success if addressed. By practising self-awareness, one can recognise these potential pitfalls and work to mitigate them. The ability to self-reflect and adjust accordingly equips individuals with a critical tool to handle adversities, an essential element of resilience.

Points to Ponder:

1. Embrace adaptability, not rigidity.
2. In every challenge lies an opportunity.
3. An unassailable position is more reliable than the enemy's indecision.
4. Leadership pitfalls can turn a victor into a victim.
5. Understanding and variation in tactics are the lifelines of successful strategy execution.

Chapter IX

Military March

> *Sun Tzu said:*
> *Generally, armies prefer high ground and dislike low ground.*
> *They value the sunny side and despise the shady side.*
> *If you can nourish your health and avoid dense areas,*
> *your army will be free from disease, and this is the way to ensure victory.*
> *In hill and dale formations,*
> *you must occupy the sunny side and protect the right side,*
> *which is advantageous for the troops and the terrain.*
> *When it rains upstream, and the water level rises,*
> *those who wish to cross must wait until it settles....*
> *When commands are consistently enforced and used to instruct the people,*
> *then the people will obey;*
> *if orders are not consistently enforced and used to guide the people, then the people will not obey.*
> *Commands that are consistently enforced will find harmony with the masses.*

In this text, Sun Tzu offers guidance on the tactical use of terrain in military operations, emphasising the preference for higher ground and the sunny side for strategic advantage and health reasons. He also highlights the importance of understanding and adapting to environmental conditions, like waiting for water levels to settle after rain before crossing.

Furthermore, Sun Tzu addresses the importance of consistent leadership and the enforcement of commands. He suggests consistency in supervision and instruction leads to obedience and harmony among the troops. This reflects his broader view on the importance of stability, predictability, and trust in military leadership.

In this chapter, Sun Tzu offers strategic insights for mobilising and positioning an army in various terrains and how to interpret the movements and behaviours of the enemy. These guidelines may apply to modern contexts like business competition, team management, and strategic decision-making.

He advises swift movement across mountains and valleys to camp in elevated, sun-facing positions for a strategic advantage. He discourages initiating conflict on mountain peaks or in mid-river. The advice applies to businesses to refrain from engaging competitors when competitors occupy high ground or in situations that leave them vulnerable. He also emphasises the importance of environmental awareness, advising to avoid natural hazards and to use such locations to trap enemies.

Sun Tzu encourages observing signs of enemy activity to predict their moves. Birds flying off, dust rising, or unnatural changes could indicate enemy advancement. Similarly, the behaviour of enemy troops, such as formation shifts or increased preparation, can reveal their intentions. In a corporate setting, a competitor's behaviour, such as market actions, team reshuffling, or sudden aggressiveness, can be signs of their strategy, enabling companies to anticipate and counteract those moves effectively.

The chapter also underscores the importance of a leader's ability to maintain discipline and morale in their troops. Effective leadership is achieved through a delicate balance of respect and control, not unlike modern management theories advocating for an empathetic yet assertive leadership style. Mistreatment or lack of discipline can lead to insubordination and ineffectiveness. Sun Tzu suggests building solid and respectful relationships with team members, ensuring clear communication, and maintaining harmony and discipline to achieve common goals in a business setting.

In essence, Sun Tzu's strategic counsel on manoeuvring, positioning, observation, and leadership in "Military March" can serve as a valuable guide for modern strategic decision-making and team management in various contexts, particularly in business competition and strategic planning.

Sun Tzu's teachings offer numerous strategic insights that can be applied in contemporary fields such as sales & marketing, human resources management, and international politics.

In sales & marketing, studying the terrain and adapting strategies in line with the market situation is essential. For instance, Apple's iPhone marketing strategy varies across geographical markets based on consumer behaviour, preferences, and competition. They adapt their messaging, pricing, and product features to suit different demands. The business strategy akins to Sun Tzu's advice on adapting to different terrains.

Similarly, Sun Tzu's advice on observing signs of enemy activity and interpreting their movements applies to competitive market analysis. Companies like Coca-Cola constantly monitor Pepsi's marketing and product launches, and vice versa, to anticipate moves and strategise their response. This mirrors Sun Tzu's counsel on using the enemy's movements to predict their actions.

Sun Tzu's insights about the importance of disciplined yet humane leadership are particularly relevant in human resources management. Google, known for its innovative HR policies, creates an environment where employees feel valued, heard, and attached to the company, promoting loyalty and discipline - echoing Sun Tzu's advice on gaining troops' trust before enforcing discipline.

Balancing firmness and empathy in leadership also applies to political leadership. For instance, New Zealand's Prime Minister Jacinda Ardern has won international praise for handling crises, from the Christchurch Mosque shootings to the COVID-19 pandemic. Her leadership style, which combines decisiveness with empathy, embodies Sun Tzu's teachings on leadership.

Sun Tzu's strategies in international politics can be seen in how countries negotiate. The recent U.S.-China trade war can be seen as both countries attempting to gain the "high ground," mirroring Sun Tzu's advice on taking the elevated, sun-facing positions. Their tactics, such as tariffs and sanctions, can be likened to Sun Tzu's advice on observing enemy behaviour and adapting one's strategy to gain an advantage.

Sun Tzu's teachings in Chapter 9 provide valuable strategic insights applicable to contemporary contexts, shaping practices in marketing, human resources, and international politics.

In addition, the episode of "Military March" also illustrates resilience concepts in adapting to the changes in environment and circumstances. Sun Tzu advises that armies should adjust their strategies according to different terrains. This flexibility and adaptability are crucial aspects of resilience. In a business context, a resilient company can adapt to market shifts or disruptions in the industry and find ways to thrive even under challenging conditions. For instance, a resilient business might pivot its product offering during a market downturn or explore new markets to maintain profitability.

Another lesson on resilience can be taken from Sun Tzu's emphasis on the good health and the well-being of the soldiers, signifying the importance of self-care and ensuring well-being. Strength is not just about surviving under stress but also about maintaining physical and mental health. In an organizational setting, this could translate into businesses prioritizing the well-being of their employees to ensure a resilient workforce that can perform optimally even under pressure or during times of change.

Lastly, Sun Tzu's advice about maintaining discipline and unity within the army underlines the power of collective resilience. In the face of challenges, a group that is united and disciplined, adhering to a common purpose, will be more resilient. An example can be a sports team that maintains unity and discipline in the face of defeat and uses these setbacks as stepping stones to improve and succeed in the future.

Sun Tzu's teachings in this chapter provide valuable insights into resilience, illustrating the importance of adaptability, self-care, and collective unity in overcoming adversity and emerging stronger from it.

Conclusion

This chapter offers comprehensive military strategies and principles, yet its essence transcends time and application, lending insight to various modern domains.

The chapter emphasises strategic adaptability, noting the importance of altering manoeuvres based on different environmental contexts. Successful leaders must understand and leverage their unique characteristics- mountains, rivers, marshes, or flat terrains. This adaptability is a vital lesson in warfare, business, interpersonal relationships, and political diplomacy, where changing circumstances demand flexibility and strategic evolution.

Furthermore, Sun Tzu places great importance on observing and interpreting signs, underscoring the need for vigilance, circumspection, and foresight. He provides a detailed guide on interpreting various signs, a practice that parallels modern competitive intelligence, where signals indicate market trends, competitor movements, or employee sentiment.

Moreover, Sun Tzu underscores the significance of the well-being and discipline of soldiers, offering an early understanding of how crucial human resource management is to any organisation's success. Leaders who treat their people with humanity yet maintain rigorous discipline will foster a mutually beneficial environment leading to victory.

In conclusion, Chapter 9 serves as a reminder of the importance of strategic flexibility, informed decision-making, and the crucial role of strong leadership in guiding teams towards success. Though rooted in military strategy, its teachings offer timeless wisdom applicable to various aspects of modern life.

Points to Ponder:

1. **Adapt to Conquer:** Underlining the importance of adjusting business strategies according to changing market environments for sustained growth.
2. **Insights Inform Success:** Encouraging vigilant observation and interpretation of market trends

and competitor actions for making informed business decisions.
3. People Power Profits: Highlighting the role of employee well-being and morale in driving business performance and profitability.
4. Discipline Directs Dominance: Stressing the significance of enforcing rules and maintaining order within organisations for efficient operations and market dominance.
5. Resilience Reaps Rewards: Emphasizing the power of business resilience and patience in navigating market challenges to secure long-term success.

Chapter X

Topography

> *Sun Tzu said:*
> *There are various types of terrain:*
> *accessible, hanging, stalemated, narrow, dangerous, and distant. ...*
> *These six principles of landscape are the general's most important responsibility,*
> *and those who lead must thoroughly understand.....*

In this excerpt, Sun Tzu categorises different terrains encountered in military campaigns and emphasises the importance of understanding these in the context of strategy and planning. Each type of terrain presents unique challenges and opportunities, and a victorious general must recognise and adapt to these:

Accessible Terrain:
Easily traversable by both sides, allowing for movement and manoeuvre.

Hanging Terrain:
Offers benefits to the first to occupy it but is challenging to hold for extended periods.

Stalemated Terrain:
It is difficult for either side to gain an advantage, often leading to a deadlock.

Narrow Terrain:

Restricted space where a smaller force can hold off a larger one.

Dangerous Terrain:
Extremely difficult or dangerous, often isolating forces and making retreat difficult.

Distant Terrain:
Far from the base of operations, posing logistical and operational challenges.

Sun Tzu's focus on terrain demonstrates his understanding of the complex interplay between geography and military tactics, where the physical environment can significantly influence the outcome of conflicts. Understanding and utilising the characteristics of the terrain are crucial elements of successful military strategy.

This Chapter explores the relationship between geographical locations and military strategy and outlines the six calamities that can befall an army due to a leader's mistakes.

Sun Tzu classifies six types of terrain and presents corresponding strategies for each. Accessible ground is free for both sides to traverse. Here, Sun Tzu advises commanders to secure high and sunny spots and guard their supply lines to achieve an advantage. In the case of entangling ground, which can be abandoned but difficult to re-occupy, the general should be prepared for an offensive or defensive strategy based on the enemy's preparedness.

Temporising ground, where neither side has a clear advantage, calls for patience and tactical retreats to lure the enemy. In narrow passes, the emphasis is on securing and firmly guarding these positions first. Precipitous heights should be occupied early, but if the enemy has seized them first, retreating and enticing the enemy away is advised. If the army is far from the enemy, provoking a battle can be disadvantageous.

On terrain, Sun Tzu addresses the six calamities that can lead to defeat, which all stem from the leader's failings:

flight - (when faced with a significantly larger force),

insubordination - (when the ranks and files are more potent than the officers),

collapse - (when officers are more robust than the subordinates),

ruin - (when higher officers act out of anger or resentment without waiting for the commander's orders),

disorganisation - (when the general's orders are unclear and there's no discipline), and

rout - (when the general underestimates the enemy's strength and doesn't strategically position his troops).

Sun Tzu stresses that a general's personality trait consists of understanding the terrain, estimating the adversary, controlling the forces, and calculating of difficulties, dangers, and distances. A general should know when to fight and when not to, irrespective of orders from the ruler. Good generals should consider their soldiers as if they were their children, earning their loyalty and courage, but they must also enforce their authority and commands effectively.

Lastly, Sun Tzu stresses the importance of knowing both the enemy's and one's capabilities and understanding the nature of the terrain to secure victory. Knowing oneself but not the other or ignoring the conditions of the landscape only leads halfway towards victory.

This chapter is also a testament to the importance of resilience in navigating life's hurdles:

Adapting to Changing Conditions: Just as different terrains require different strategies, resilience requires adaptability to changing circumstances. In business or personal life, resilience means not being stuck in one problem-solving method but adapting one's approach to suit the current situation.

Learning from Mistakes: Sun Tzu outlines six calamities that can befall an army due to the general's mistakes. Resilience is about learning from mistakes, owning them, and taking steps to prevent them from happening again. It also means not being discouraged by these mistakes but viewing them as opportunities for learning and growth.

Perseverance in Difficult Circumstances: Sun Tzu's advice to occupy challenging terrains like narrow passes and steep heights reflects the quality of resilience. It symbolises determination and tenacity in the face of hardship.

Patient Strategising: This chapter suggests that patience and strategic retreat in the face of superior forces or unfavourable conditions can eventually lead to success. It is a significant component of resilience - the ability to "weather the storm" and wait for the right opportunity.

Care for People: Sun Tzu stresses the importance of treating soldiers like one's children. In a modern context, resilient leaders should care for their team, fostering a supportive environment that promotes resilience at all levels.

Self-Awareness: The final lines of the chapter reiterate the importance of "know thyself" and your enemy. Resilience often comes from solid self-awareness - understanding one's strengths, weaknesses, and the reality of the situation. This awareness enables one to withstand challenges and bounce back from setbacks more effectively.

The strategic use of terrain and understanding one's position have broad applications in various fields of contemporary life, such as marketing and sales management, human resources management, and world politics & international relations.

Marketing and Sales Management

The concept of "Topography" in Sun Tzu's philosophy can be compared to the market landscape in business. Different market conditions require unique strategies for success.

<u>Accessible ground:</u> In marketing terms, this could refer to a market segment that is easily accessible to your business and your competitors. The advantage here is the one who can occupy the "raised and sunny spots" first - those who can effectively position their product or service in the market and secure reliable supply chains and distribution channels. Apple was not the first to market with a smartphone or a tablet. Yet, they occupied the "raised and sunny spots" by differentiating their products with sleek design, intuitive interfaces, and a brand emphasising innovation and quality.

<u>Entangling ground:</u> This could be a market segment that, once entered, is difficult to exit - like subscription services or long-term contracts. If a business can attract customers into these "entangling" deals, it can secure a steady revenue stream. Apple's ecosystem of devices and services creates a sticky customer experience. Once a customer buys an Apple product, they're more likely to purchase more due to the seamless integration across devices.

<u>Temporising ground:</u> In a market with a standoff with a competitor, a business may need to wait patiently for the right opportunity to act. It could mean holding off on a product launch until the competitor reveals its hand, allowing you to respond more effectively.

<u>Narrow passes and precipitous heights</u> refer to highly specialised market segments or niches. If a

company can become a market leader in such a niche, it can essentially control access to it, making it difficult for competitors to gain a foothold.

<u>Positions far from the enemy</u> can refer to new markets or demographics your competitors have yet to target. Entering these markets can be risky but also very rewarding.

Human Resources Management:

Sun Tzu's teachings in this chapter may also apply to human resource management. The management of people in an organisation is akin to a general leading his soldiers on different terrains. Google is well-known for its people management and HR strategies, reflecting some of Sun Tzu's philosophies.

<u>Regard your soldiers as your children:</u> In HR, this is akin to treating employees with respect and care. A supportive work environment fosters higher employee engagement and loyalty, which leads to higher productivity. Google provides an environment where employees feel cared for, with benefits such as free meals, fitness centres, and opportunities for personal and professional development.

<u>Understanding capabilities and limitations:</u> Just as a general need to understand the capabilities of his soldiers and the limits of the terrain, an HR manager must understand the skills, abilities, and limitations of their staff to deploy them where they can succeed effectively.

<u>Clear Communication:</u> Clear and distinct orders are crucial in war, as they are in a business environment. The HR department is critical for ensuring that communication within the organisation is effective and that roles and expectations are clearly defined.

World Politics & International Relations:

In global politics and international relations, strategically using "topography" can refer to a country's geopolitical advantages and disadvantages.

<u>Narrow passes:</u> The Suez Canal, controlled by Egypt, serves as a strategic global shipping lane, demonstrating the geopolitical significance of maintaining such "narrow passes". So are the Strait of Hormuz in the Persian Gulf and the Malacca Strait in Southeast Asia. Countries that control these "narrow passes" have a strategic advantage.

<u>Great distances from the enemy:</u> This could refer to the geopolitical isolation of certain countries, which may be advantageous in terms of security but could be a disadvantage in trade and diplomacy. Australia, for instance, provides it with a measure of security but also poses challenges in terms of trade and diplomatic relations, as it's distanced from major global players.

<u>Knowing when to fight:</u> Sun Tzu advises that one should only engage in battle when victory is certain. This could be considered a caution against entering conflicts or negotiations without a clear advantage or strategy in international relations.

Respecting one's adversary: This is reflected in diplomatic strategies. For example, despite its economic and political differences, the U.S. initiated a dialogue with North Korea under President Donald Trump's administration, recognising the need to understand and negotiate with its adversary to achieve its diplomatic objectives.

Preparedness and Flexibility: Sun Tzu advocates understanding the different terrains and adjusting strategies accordingly. This can be interpreted as being prepared and flexible, two critical aspects of resilience. However, while this offers a method to avoid adverse situations, resilience also involves managing and recovering from setbacks when they occur.

Avoiding Conflict: Sun Tzu's teachings advocate avoiding unnecessary battles if they are not advantageous. This could be criticised for its cautiousness, as resilience often involves confronting challenges head-on. By avoiding conflict, individuals and organisations may miss opportunities to build strength through learning and growth.

The Dehumanisation of the Army: Although Sun Tzu suggests regarding your soldiers as your children, this approach has a strategic underpinning. The soldiers are tools to achieve victory in his context. The modern concept of resilience, especially in HR, focuses on the individual's psychological well-being and personal growth, which goes beyond this utilitarian perspective.

Reactive vs Proactive Approach: Sun Tzu's teachings in this chapter suggest a reactive approach -

adapting to the existing terrain or circumstance. While adaptability is vital to resilience, one should also emphasise the proactive aspect of building strength by fostering personal growth, strengthening relationships, and creating a positive environment.

Conclusion

In conclusion, the episode "Topography" presents pivotal stratagems for the field of war and, by extension, the complex arena of life. It offers a robust framework to navigate any situation, whether a military confrontation or a boardroom dispute. This episode provides timeless insights into the art of resilience.

The essence of any strategy lies in an in-depth understanding of the battlefield. This idea suggests that we delve deeply into the complexities of our environments, analysing and comprehending all facets to devise the most successful strategy. Grasping the intricacies of the surroundings equips one to anticipate and plan for future challenges rather than merely reacting to them.

Simultaneously, it is vital to discern battles that are worth fighting from those that are not. The courage to step back from an unwinnable fight is often more valuable than reckless bravery.

A leader who engenders a strong sense of belonging and trust in his team inspires loyalty, ensuring team members stand united, even in the face of daunting challenges. The leader's ability to establish such a familial bond significantly boosts the team's resilience and effectiveness.

To underscore the potential catastrophes spawned from mismanagement, a clear command structure and a well-organised team are the foundations of efficient execution. Disorder and confusion are the enemies of success and can derail even the most well-thought-out plans.

Lastly, Sun Tzu culminates this wisdom-laden chapter with a powerful axiom: To guarantee victory, one must thoroughly know oneself, the enemy, and the terrain. This profound understanding translates into a tactical advantage, allowing us to effectively counteract our foes and leverage the terrain's quirks to our benefit.

Points to ponder:

1. Know the battlefield, win the battle.
2. Avoid the fight you can't win.
3. Foster loyalty, command respect.
4. Mismanagement breeds disaster.
5. Know yourself, know the enemy, and know the topography.

Chapter XI

Nine Types of Grounds

> *Sun Tzu said:*
> *In the art of war, there are different types of ground: Dispersive, marginal, contentious, open, intersecting, critical, complex, surrounded, and desperate....*
> *Therefore, on dispersive ground, do not fight;*
> *on marginal ground, do not stop;*
> *on the contentious ground, do not attack;*
> *on open ground, do not cut off your retreat;*
> *on the intersecting ground, make connections;*
> *on the critical ground, plunder;*
> *on difficult ground, keep moving;*
> *on surrounded ground, plan;*
> *on desperate ground, fight.....*

In this text, Sun Tzu describes nine types of terrain, each with its strategic considerations. Each type of ground requires a different approach, and understanding these principles is key to applying effective military strategies. Sun Tzu emphasises the need for flexibility and adaptability in response to the terrain and circumstances.

Sun Tzu emphasises the importance of seizing the initiative and acting quickly, using all possible means to mislead the enemy, and maintaining morale among one's troops. He suggests leading soldiers into situations where retreat is not an option, as it will encourage them to fight more fiercely.

To start with, I wish to draw parallels between Sun Tzu's teachings in "The Art of War" and contemporary business or international politics contexts:

Disperse: This is analogous to a company operating within its home market, where it knows the ins and outs of the environment, the demands, the competition, and the regulatory landscape. Focusing on growth and expansion is often more advantageous than engaging in a head-on competition that can erode resources. In the international political arena, it could mean a country's territory where diplomatic or internal issues are better solved peacefully rather than going into conflict.

Marginal: This could be seen as a business entering a new market. It's not wise to halt but to keep moving and understanding the environment better, akin to consistently gaining market share. In international politics, when a country makes diplomatic inroads into another's territory, it should keep fostering better relations rather than pausing.

Contentious: It might represent a lucrative but highly competitive market segment in business. Attacking head-on might not be beneficial as it could lead to price wars or loss of resources. It could refer to disputed territories where direct conflict can lead to heavy losses and international repercussions.

Open: In a market with many competitors and no dominant players, a business should not block competitors' strategies but instead focus on carving its niche. In politics, open dialogue between nations in a neutral forum without attempting to suppress each other's viewpoints can often lead to more beneficial outcomes.

Intersecting: This situation could represent business sectors where partnerships and collaborations can lead to mutual growth. In politics, it could mean a region where several nations have interests, and diplomacy and alliances become crucial.

Critical: For businesses, this might be operating in a tough foreign market where securing supply chains and resources is vital. In politics, it could represent a situation where a country has military forces deep in enemy territory, needing secure lines of supplies and communication.

Difficult: These could refer to businesses in very challenging market conditions, such as a monopoly or regulatory pressure. They must resort to strategic decisions, innovation, and differentiation to survive and thrive. Similarly, in politics, it could refer to situations of diplomatic isolation or economic sanctions where strategic alliances and negotiations are vital.

Surrounded: This could refer to businesses in challenging market conditions, such as a monopoly or regulatory pressure. They must resort to strategic decisions, innovation, and differentiation to survive and thrive. Similarly, in politics, it could refer to situations of diplomatic isolation or economic sanctions where strategic alliances and negotiations are vital.

Desperate: When there is no choice but to fight for survival.

In essence, this episode is about understanding your environment, the state of your troops, and how to use all possible and available means to seize opportunities and ultimately achieve victory. For this, I wish to further elaborate Sun Tzu's "Nine Types of Grounds" in terms of Sales & Marketing, Human Resources Management, and International Politics below:

Sales & Marketing

Disperse: Similar to familiar markets where a company operates. The caution against fighting could mean starting pricing wars with competitors in markets where you already have a strong presence, which is unnecessary.

Marginal: When entering a new market, quickly establish your presence and make your brand known to gain a foothold.

Contentious: In markets where competition is fierce, it may only sometimes be advisable to be aggressive in advertising and promotions. Sometimes, a more subtle, strategic approach can be more effective.

Open: This could represent an open market with many competitors. Finding a unique, distinctive way to reach customers rather than directly competing with all other brands may be more beneficial.

Intersecting: Strategic partnerships or alliances can be advantageous in a market with many competitors.

Difficult: Innovative strategies and niche marketing can be the key to survival and growth for smaller companies in a market dominated by multinational corporations.

Human Resources Management

Dispersive: In HR, this is analogous to time to give staff members a push or a pat on the back to keep them going forward and moving forward to achieve better results. Sometimes, a manager has to inspire team members to perform better.

Marginal: This might apply when introducing new policies or changes. It is important not to pause but to continue driving change.

Contentious: This could refer to situations such as layoffs or restructures requiring sensitive handling.

Intersecting: When an organisation goes through a crisis or downsizing, HR must resort to strategic planning and execution.

Desperate: This could refer to the high-pressure, high-stakes periods in an organisation's life where HR must motivate and engage employees to commit fully to their tasks.

International Politics & Relations:

Dispersive: This could represent a nation's domestic policies, where the leader must maintain unity and harmony.

Marginal: Diplomatic incursions into other territories require caution and strategy.

Contentious: This could represent a nation's domestic policies, where the leader must maintain unity and harmony.

Open: This could represent international arenas, like the UN, where diplomacy and dialogue are essential.

Intersecting: This might represent areas or issues of common interest to many nations, where building alliances can be advantageous.

Desperate: During war or severe conflict, a country must fully mobilise its resources and resort to every available strategy to ensure survival.

Sun Tzu's general advice to maintain flexibility, act quickly and decisively, use deception when advantageous, understand the environment, and motivate your troops (or employees or allies) applies to many contexts.

The following examples demonstrate how Sun Tzu's principles continue to have relevance today in various fields, aiding strategic decisions and actions even in contemporary scenarios:

<u>Sales & Marketing:</u> Apple Inc., under Steve Jobs, displayed a strong understanding of the "intersecting highways" principle. The launch of the iPhone was a strategic move that intersected telecommunications, internet accessibility, and personal entertainment into one device. The product effectively seized control of multiple markets simultaneously, dominating "key ground" and disrupting the balance of power in the tech industry.

<u>International Politics & Relations:</u> The Cold War era demonstrates Sun Tzu's "contentious ground" principle. The U.S. and the Soviet Union, although never engaged in direct warfare, continually vied for advantageous positions on the global stage. The space race, for instance, was a clear strategic move by both nations to secure a favourable place in terms of technological superiority and international prestige.

The Art of Resilience

Resilience, the ability to withstand stresses and pressures, is a fundamental theme throughout Sun Tzu's "Nine Types of Grounds". He emphasises that the capability to adapt and respond strategically to different circumstances is critical to achieving victory. Here's how these teachings relate to resilience.

1. Disperse Ground: Resilience often means maintaining unity and purpose even in familiar and comfortable situations. It involves the ability to remain vigilant and avoid complacency.
2. Marginal Ground: Resilience involves adapting quickly to new situations and conditions. Once you've moved into unfamiliar territory, don't halt; quickly adjust and establish a foothold.
3. Contentious Ground: In situations with potential for conflict or contention, resilience means not being reactionary. Instead, thoughtful, strategic decision-making ensures long-term survival and success.
4. Open Ground: Resilience involves being able to manage situations where there is a lot of freedom of movement and many possibilities. It means being adaptive and flexible rather than rigidly trying to control everything.
5. Intersecting Ground: This emphasises the resilience of alliances and partnerships. When you're in a position where many paths converge, you can strengthen your strength by joining others.
6. Contentious Ground: Sun Tzu advises gathering resources deep into enemy territory, emphasising the importance of resourcefulness, a critical aspect of resilience.

7. Open Ground: Resilience involves persevering in the face of obstacles and moving forward.
8. Surrounded Ground: When in a position where you're restricted or cornered, resilience means using strategy and guile to turn the situation around.
9. Desperate Ground: In situations where survival is at stake, resilience takes the form of an unwavering will to fight and survive, regardless of how dire the circumstances may appear.

Conclusion

"Nine Types of Grounds" offers a comprehensive strategy guide for leaders in varying scenarios. Each situation: dispersive, facile, contentious, open, intersecting highways, profound, challenging, hemmed-in, and desperate ground, represents a distinct context requiring a unique approach and strategy. Sun Tzu's wisdom lies in identifying these grounds and providing the corresponding method to navigate them effectively.

In the dispersive ground, which is analogous to fighting in familiar territory, the key is maintaining unity of purpose. Facile ground requires quick adaptation and swift action. Contentious ground, valuable to both sides in a conflict, demands careful and strategic decision-making rather than impulsivity. Open ground, offering liberty of movement, necessitates adaptability and flexibility. Forging alliances and partnerships are encouraged.

The severe ground scenario highlights the importance of resourcefulness. Difficult ground, representing challenging circumstances, underscores the need for continuous movement despite obstacles. Encircled ground advises resorting to cunning and strategic planning when trapped or cornered. In contrast, deadly ground calls for unrelenting courage and a relentless will to fight when survival is at stake.

Sun Tzu's teaching ultimately emphasises strategic resilience and adaptability according to the situation. The core principles revolve around understanding the dynamics of the environment, the judicious use of resources, creating unity among the ranks, and strategic manoeuvring.

Essentially, the "Nine Types of Grounds" serve as a timeless guide, offering leaders critical insights on navigating various challenges and securing victory - whether in the military, business, or politics. The wisdom transcends the bounds of warfare, offering enduring, universal lessons on strategy, leadership, and resilience.

Points to Ponder:

1. Recognise your Ground: Understand the intricacies of your situation.
2. Unity and Adaptability: Unity and Flexibility are the cornerstones of survival and success.
3. Strategic Alliances: Diplomacy and Partnerships are as crucial as combat readiness.
4. Resourcefulness and Perseverance: Persistence pays.
5. From the depths of desperation often springs the resilience that leads to great triumphs.

Chapter XII

Fire Attack

> *Sun Tzu said:*
> *Generally, there are five types of fire attacks:*
> *Setting fire to personnel,*
> *Setting fire to stores,*
> *Setting fire to transport equipment,*
> *Setting fire to arsenals and*
> *Setting fire to the enemy's formations.....*

In this excerpt, Sun Tzu outlines the different strategies for using fire as a weapon in warfare. Each method targets a specific aspect of the enemy's resources or forces:

Setting fire to personnel: involves direct attacks on enemy soldiers, aiming to cause chaos and disrupt their formations.

Setting fire to stores: Targeting the enemy's supply depots, which can cripple their ability to sustain their troops.

Setting fire to transport equipment: Destroying the enemy's transportation means, such as wagons or beasts of burden, to disrupt their mobility and supply lines.

Setting fire to arsenals: Attacking the enemy's stockpiles of weapons and ammunition reduces their capability to wage war.

Setting fire to the enemy's formations: Directly targeting the enemy's organised units, disrupting their battle plans and causing disarray.

Sun Tzu's discussion of fire attacks reflects his understanding of using environmental and psychological factors in warfare, aiming to weaken the enemy by targeting critical logistical and operational elements.

Timing is critical when using fire, ideally when the weather is dry and the wind is rising. The materials for starting a fire should always be ready.

There are five possible scenarios when attacking with fire, each requiring a different response. If a fire starts in the enemy's camp, it's time to attack. If a fire breaks out, but the enemy remains calm, wait. When the fire is at its peak, follow it with an attack if possible. If it's possible to start a fire from outside, don't wait for one to begin inside. When creating a fire, always do so from the upwind side. Understanding these scenarios, observing the stars, and timing attacks for the good days are all part of intelligent warfare. Water can also provide an advantage in battle by blocking the enemy, though it can't deprive them of all resources.

Winning battles requires a spirit of enterprise. Acting without it can lead to stagnation and wasted time. The wise ruler and good general plan and prepare well in advance. Troops should only be deployed and battles fought if an advantage is gained, the situation is critical, and emotions are controlled. Impulsive or angry decisions can lead to irreversible losses, like the destruction of a kingdom or death. Therefore, an enlightened ruler is careful, ensuring peace in the country and maintaining an entire army.

Sun Tzu's "Fire Attack" strategies apply in various modern contexts, including warfare, business (sales & marketing), human resources management, and politics. The book's teachings focus on strategy, preparation, understanding the "enemy" (or competitor), and environment, which can be applied beyond traditional warfare. Here are a few examples:

Modern Warfare: Modern warfare isn't typically characterised by the literal use of fire as a weapon, but Sun Tzu's principles are still applicable. For example, "setting fire to stores" could be interpreted as disrupting an enemy's supply chain or communications in a cyber warfare context.

Sales & Marketing: The principle of striking at the enemy's weak point or when unprepared can be applied here. A business can "attack" a competitor when they're feeble (e.g., during a reputational crisis) or off guard (e.g., by launching a new product that it cannot easily match). Also, understanding the "right timing" to launch a campaign can be derived from "the proper season" and "special days" for starting a conflagration.

Human Resources Management: HR managers can use Sun Tzu's strategies by identifying "critical positions" (important roles or key personnel) and ensuring competent people fill them. Additionally, managing emotions and avoiding impulsive decisions (Sun Tzu's caution against fighting out of anger) is crucial in conflict resolution and negotiations in HR.

Politics: Politics often involves strategic planning, foresight, and calculated moves, very much like a game of chess or a war scenario. Sun Tzu's advice to act only when there is an advantage, not out of anger or pique, can be used in political strategies, negotiations, or international diplomacy.

While the specific tactics Sun Tzu described may not always directly apply, the principles underlying his strategies - understanding the opponent, taking advantage of timing and environment, and careful planning - remain relevant across various fields.

Resilience is a core theme throughout Sun Tzu's "The Art of War". Although not explicitly mentioned in Chapter 12, "Fire Attack", the principles of resilience can be derived from several of Sun Tzu's strategies. Here's how:

Preparation and Planning: Sun Tzu emphasises the importance of planning and preparing ahead, which builds resilience by ensuring one is ready to deal with difficulties or setbacks. For example, having a backup plan or resources can help you bounce back quickly if an initial method fails.

Understanding the Environment: Sun Tzu stresses the need to understand and adapt to the environment (including weather conditions and the position of the stars in Chapter 12). In a modern context, this can be seen as adapting to changing market conditions, policy shifts, or social trends.

Knowing When To Act and When Not To: Sun Tzu's advice only to move when there is an advantage and to hold back when there isn't can be seen as a resilience strategy. By conserving resources and energy until they can be most effectively used, one can remain strong and continue striving towards their goals even in adverse conditions.

Emotional Control: Sun Tzu advises against acting out of anger or spite, suggesting that leaders remain calm and patient. This emotional resilience allows one to make rational decisions even in challenging or stressful circumstances.

In the modern context, whether in business, personal lives, politics, or other fields, resilience remains crucial for success. Although written in a different era and for warfare, Sun Tzu's principles offer valuable insights into building and maintaining strength.

Conclusion

Chapter 12 discusses the strategic use of fire in warfare and lays out the fundamental principles for its use. He provides practical advice on when and how to effectively utilise fire as a weapon, emphasising the importance of preparation, understanding the environment, and careful timing. The chapter also underscores the strategic response to different scenarios and warns against hasty or emotion-driven decisions, emphasising the potentially irreversible consequences of such actions.

While Sun Tzu's specific tactics for using fire in war are tied to a different era, the underlying principles remain relevant. They can apply to various modern contexts, including but not limited to business strategy, politics, human resources management, and personal decision-making. The emphasis on careful planning, adaptability, and strategic action underscores the importance of wisdom, foresight, and resilience, essential for successful leadership and effective strategy in any field.

In conclusion, Sun Tzu's Chapter 12 provides timeless wisdom that may overcome challenges, seize opportunities, and succeed in different aspects of contemporary life when interpreted metaphorically and strategically.

Points to Ponder

1. Strategise with fire and win with intelligence and strength.
2. Timing and environment fuel the flame of victory.
3. When emotion rises, wisdom falls.
4. Attack not from anger but from an advantage.
5. Prepare, observe, adapt – the triumvirate of triumph.

Chapter XIII

Employing Espionage

Sun Tzu said:
There are five types of intelligence operations: Local Agents, Inside Agents, Double Agents, Doomed Agents, and Surviving Agents.....

In this chapter, Sun Tzu describes different methods of espionage and intelligence gathering, each serving a specific purpose:

Local Agents (Residents): People from the enemy's territory or local area who provide intelligence based on their familiarity with the region.

Inside Agents (Infiltrators): People within the enemy's administration or inner circle can provide confidential information.

Double Agents: These agents work ostensibly for the enemy but report back to their original employer, providing critical insights about the enemy's plans.

Doomed Agents: They are knowingly given misleading information, which they then pass to the enemy, intended to deceive and misdirect.

Surviving Agents: These spies are tasked with entering the enemy's camp, gathering direct intelligence, and returning with this valuable information.

Sun Tzu explains the indispensable role of espionage in warfare. He highlights the gravity of ignorance about the enemy's condition. He declares it as the pinnacle of inhumanity, detrimental to the army and the nation's resources and populace. War is both a domestic and foreign issue, draining significant resources and causing profound disturbances in a state's economy and the lives of its people. A protracted war leads to fatigue and exhaustion, hampering productivity on a large scale.

According to Sun Tzu, the key to victory lies in foreknowledge, which transcends the capabilities of an ordinary leader. This foreknowledge, he explains, cannot be gleaned from spirits, experiential inferences, or logical deductions but exclusively from the intelligence gathered about enemy dispositions through human sources. This understanding underscores the criticality of using agents in warfare.

Maintaining intimate relations with agents is of the utmost importance for the army, asserts Sun Tzu. Agents require liberal rewards, and their operations should be enveloped in the greatest secrecy. Their usefulness depends on intuitive sagacity, and their handling requires benevolence and honesty. The accurate interpretation of their reports requires a subtle, ingenious mind. Agents are to be utilised in all matters, their secrets protected with the utmost caution, and death is the penalty for premature divulgence of information.

Knowledge of their inner circle and primary personnel is necessary to conquer an enemy effectively. Agents are instrumental in this task. Converted agents, in particular, serve as the foundation of the spying system, helping recruit local and inward spies, manipulating doomed spies to spread misinformation, and deploying surviving spies at opportune moments. Therefore, they should be treated with extreme generosity.

Sun Tzu emphasises the role of agents as vital in warfare as the mobility and strategies of a military rely heavily on the information they provide. One striking example that illustrates the strategic use of agents is the case of the Cambridge Spy Ring during the Cold War - Kim Philby, Donald Maclean, Guy Burges, and Anthony Blunt. Kim Philby is the most well-known member of this group. He worked for Britain's Secret Intelligence Service (MI6) and later became the head of the counter-intelligence division, where his job was to hunt for Soviet spies. However, unknown to his superiors, he was an agent for the Soviet Union. Philby managed to pass significant amounts of intelligence to the Soviets, including crucial information during World War II and the early stages of the Cold War.

The principles and wisdom conveyed in Sun Tzu's teachings on espionage and foreknowledge apply beyond warfare's confines. These principles can be adapted to modern business and commerce, as obtaining information and gaining insights into the competition, market trends, and consumer behaviours are critical for strategic planning and decision-making.

<u>Market Research (Local Agents):</u> Businesses often utilise market surveys and research to understand and gain insights about their customers and competitors.

They gather information about market trends, customer preferences, and competitor strategies to make informed decisions. A real-life example can be seen in how Starbucks conducts comprehensive market research before entering a new geographical area, understanding local tastes, preferences, and cultural nuances - much like Sun Tzu's "local agents."

Industry Insiders (Inside Agentss): Many businesses employ industry insiders or experts with a deep understanding of the competitors' strategies and inner workings. For instance, Apple famously hired John Sculley, the former CEO of PepsiCo, as their CEO in the 1980s to leverage his experience and insights into marketing and consumer products.

Converted Agents: In the corporate world, converted spies could be likened to hiring employees from competitors, who bring with them insights about the operations, strategies, and tactics of the rival firm. In 2010, Google's then-employee, Marissa Mayer, moved to Yahoo and became its CEO, bringing along her insights and experiences from Google.

Corporate Espionage (Doomed Agentss): Although not encouraged or ethical, instances of corporate espionage are not unheard of. Misinformation can be used to lead competitors astray. For example, in the auto industry, companies often disguise upcoming models during testing to mislead competitors - an act similar to using Sun Tzu's "doomed agents".

Surviving Agents: These can be akin to companies maintaining a long-term view of the market and competitors. For instance, Microsoft was able to pivot and transform itself under the leadership of Satya Nadella by closely monitoring trends in the tech industry and reinventing its strategies based on these insights.

Remember that while Sun Tzu's teachings offer valuable strategic insights, it's essential to consider them in the light of ethics and legality, especially in a business context. Like a good general, a good business leader should always strive to act ethically and responsibly.

The teachings in this chapter have relevance to the concept of resilience, especially in terms of strategic resilience. In a broader sense, resilience is the capacity to recover quickly from difficulties, adapt to change, and keep going in the face of adversity.

Understanding the Environment (Foreknowledge): Sun Tzu underscores the importance of understanding the enemy's condition. This can be likened to understanding the risks, threats, and opportunities in a business environment or any other adversarial situation. A resilient organisation or individual can effectively utilise this foreknowledge to adapt strategies, make informed decisions, and navigate adversities.

Using Spies (Information Gathering): Sun Tzu's use of agents for gathering information can be metaphorically extended to modern resilience-building techniques. This involves active monitoring of the environment, acquiring knowledge about potential risks, and preparing for them proactively. For instance, a company can stay resilient by keeping an eye on market trends, evolving customer preferences, and competitor strategies, allowing it to adapt quickly and effectively.

Investment in Intelligence (Valuing Information): Sun Tzu emphasises rewarding spies generously and understanding the value they provide. In terms of resilience, this teaches us to invest in intelligence, knowledge, and skills to navigate changes effectively. This could involve investing in training and development for individuals or organisations to equip them better to handle challenges.

Flexibility (Adaptability): Sun Tzu refers to different types of spies that can be seen as different strategies or approaches to a situation. This illustrates the need for flexibility and adaptability, critical elements of resilience. It reminds us to use various methods and be ready to change our strategy based on new information or changing circumstances.

Secrecy and Sagacity (Preparedness and Wisdom): The need for secrecy and intuitive sagacity in dealing with spies highlights the importance of preparedness and wisdom in resilience. This involves being ready for potential threats and having the insight to understand and interpret the information to make effective decisions correctly.

In essence, the principles in this chapter teach us to stay informed, be adaptable, understand the value of knowledge, and be prepared - all of which contribute to building resilience.

Conclusion:
Unlocking Sun Tzu's Wisdom for Modern Challenges

While initially intended for warfare, Sun Tzu's teachings in Chapter 13 provide valuable insights that encourage a positive and proactive attitude towards life. His emphasis on foreknowledge, the value of information, adaptability, and preparedness are all vital principles that lead to success in adversarial situations and contribute to personal growth and the development of a resilient character.

Understanding our environment and its dynamics empowers us to make informed decisions, adapt to changes, and navigate life's challenges more effectively. Gathering information, staying informed, and valuing knowledge equip us with the tools needed to understand the world around us better and, as a result, interact with it more effectively.

Sun Tzu's teachings encourage flexibility and adaptability, traits that are valuable not only in a battlefield context but also in life. Adapting to different situations, learning from various experiences, and being flexible in our approaches are the keys to surviving and thriving in a world of constant change.

Moreover, Sun Tzu's importance on preparedness and wisdom reminds us that life, like a battlefield, is entirely uncertain. However, we can face any challenge head-on by staying prepared, making wise choices, and learning from our experiences.

In conclusion, Sun Tzu's teachings in this chapter offer a blueprint for a proactive life approach. They encourage us to stay informed, be adaptable, value knowledge, and prepare for the unexpected. By incorporating these principles, we can become more resilient, turn adversities into opportunities, and lead a more fulfilling and successful life. Embrace life as a continuous learning journey, stay prepared for the battles it may present, and remember - in every challenge lies an opportunity for growth and triumph.

Points to Ponder:

1. Knowledge is Power: Stay Informed, Stay Ahead.
2. Adapt and Overcome: Embrace Change, Seize Opportunities.
3. Invest in Intelligence: Value Information, Shape Destiny.
4. Preparation Meets Opportunity: Stay Ready, Never Get Caught off-guard.
5. Master the Art of Flexibility: Change Tactics, Win Battles.

Epilogue

People often liken the business world to a battlefield, and it's not uncommon to see examples of military tactics and war strategies that may apply to businesses. Bill Gates, the founder of Microsoft, once recommended "The Art of War" by Sun Tzu on GatesNotes as a must-read. Sun Tzu's principles of avoiding conflict, causing no harm, and benefitting oneself while benefiting others align closely with contemporary business philosophy, emphasising competition and cooperation.

Coca-Cola has become the world's largest beverage company, marketing in over 200 countries and selling 1.8 billion drinks daily through a localised strategy. This approach originated during World War II when then-CEO Robert Woodruff desired that every U.S. soldier worldwide could have access to Coca-Cola. However, realising that relying solely on production and delivery from the U.S. would not meet global demand, he began to promote the "Think Global, Act Local" strategy. Coca-Cola embodies the principle: "The skilled leader in war feeds off the enemy's land. He does not rely on his home base for supplies. This way, his army's food is sufficient."

In this epilogue, I wish to draw readers' attention to the following examples that may align, if not exemplify, Sun Tzu's teachings:

Dyson

While it might seem a bit far-fetched at first glance, it's possible to draw parallels between the strategies found in Sun Tzu's "The Art of War" and the way Dyson approaches the marketing and innovation of their cordless vacuum cleaners:

Know yourself and know your enemy: Sun Tzu suggested that understanding oneself and the competition is crucial to victory. Dyson has adopted this principle by conducting in-depth market research. They know their strengths - innovation, design, and technology - and they also make it a point to understand their competitors' products and strategies, which enables them to create superior products that meet customer needs more effectively.

Plan Strategically and Take the Whole into Account: Dyson didn't just create a cordless vacuum cleaner - they innovated and redesigned the entire concept of vacuum cleaners. They considered the whole landscape of the product, not just one element, similar to how a military strategist would consider all facets of warfare.

The Element of Surprise: Sun Tzu often talked about the value of surprising one's enemies. Surprise may translate to releasing groundbreaking, unexpected products or features in a business context. Dyson has been known for its surprise factor, as they often introduce products that exceed customer expectations and lcapfrog competitors' capabilities.

Value of Speed: In the "Art of War," the importance of speed in warfare is highlighted. Similarly, Dyson's ability to rapidly innovate, design, and bring products to market enables them to stay ahead of their competition. They are often first to market with new technology, giving them a competitive advantage.

Topography (Market): Sun Tzu stressed using the terrain to one's advantage in a war. Similarly, Dyson identified the unique landscape of the home appliance market, where consumers value design as much as functionality. Dyson's products stand out in design, which makes them attractive to the consumer, giving them an advantage over competitors.

Morale and Leadership: Just like soldiers' morale can determine the outcome of battles, employees' morale can significantly impact a company's success.

Remember, though, that while it's interesting to draw these comparisons, Dyson's success is likely more directly attributable to effective modern business strategies and practices, strong leadership, and a commitment to research and development rather than ancient warfare strategies.

Tesla

However, Sun Tzu's principles have indeed stood the test of time, and one may apply them in various contexts in business. Just as with the previous example of Dyson, it's possible to apply principles from Sun Tzu's "The Art of War" to understand some of the strategies used by Elon Musk's Tesla. Remember that these are primarily interpretations and comparisons rather than direct applications.

Know Yourself and Know Your Enemy: Tesla has a clear understanding of its strengths: electric vehicle technology, self-driving features, and high-performance cars, all underpinned by a strong brand image. Tesla also has a keen sense of the competition, often being compared to legacy automakers as well as up-and-coming EV manufacturers. Tesla's competitive edge is maintained by constantly innovating and improving its products and technologies.

Win Without Fighting: Tesla has positioned itself so it doesn't directly compete with traditional automakers. Instead of fighting these companies on the ground (combustion engines), Tesla pioneered a relatively untapped market: electric vehicles. Tesla effectively "won" by changing the rules of the game.

Strategic Depth: Tesla's decision to build its Supercharger network ensures a new way of securing its "supply lines" - similar to how a military commander would ensure a secure supply line in warfare. This Supercharger network is one of Tesla's significant strengths and provides a unique vehicle selling point.

The Chain of Command: Sun Tzu highlighted the importance of unity in leadership. With Musk at the helm, Tesla has a clear and unified vision. His charismatic and robust oversight and ability to communicate this vision to his team and the public have been integral to Tesla's success.

Speed and Preparation: Similar to how quick responsiveness can be advantageous in warfare, Tesla's approach to rapid innovation and iteration of its products allows it to stay ahead of competitors. This is evident in the frequent over-the-air software updates that Tesla vehicles receive, constantly improving and adding new features.

Employing Espionage (Intelligence): Sun Tzu emphasised the importance of gathering intelligence. While Tesla doesn't use "spies," it heavily relies on data collected from its fleet of vehicles to improve its technologies, particularly in autonomous driving.

Marketing and Perception: Sun Tzu wrote about the power of perception in warfare. Tesla, and Musk in particular, are adept at managing public perception. Tesla's minimalistic marketing approach and Musk's extensive use of social media have helped create a powerful and attractive brand image.

Again, while these principles can offer exciting ways to look at Tesla's strategies, they are an interpretation. Tesla's success is primarily due to its innovative technology, effective leadership, and successful marketing approaches.

Donald Trump

While Sun Tzu's "The Art of War" was written with military strategy in mind, many have found its principles applicable to various fields, including politics. While it is unknown whether Donald Trump intentionally applied Sun Tzu's approach during his 2016 presidential campaign, there are certain similarities. Here are a few examples:

The Element of Surprises: Trump's campaign often made unexpected moves and statements that drew media attention, continually surprising the public and his opponents. The strategy aligns with Sun Tzu's tactic of unpredictability and use of surprise to keep opponents off balance.

Know Yourself and Know Your Enemy: Trump keenly understood his voter base, used simple language and addressed topics that resonated with them. At the same time, he was adept at highlighting the perceived weaknesses of his opponents.

Strategic Withdrawal: There were moments when Trump seemed to back down or withdraw from certain controversies or confrontations, only to re-engage later when the circumstances were more favourable. Sun Tzu advises knowing when to fight and when not to fight.

Winning Hearts and Minds: Sun Tzu emphasised the importance of maintaining the troops' morale. Trump could rally his supporters with his messages, keeping them enthusiastic and engaged.

Employing Espionage (Information): In The Art of War, Sun Tzu underlines the importance of intelligence and information in winning battles. While not using "spies" per se, Trump's campaign used data, public sentiment, and media trends to adapt their strategies accordingly.

Strategic Attack: Sun Tzu believed in winning battles with the least possible effort. Trump's frequent use of Twitter was a way of reaching millions of people directly, with a minimum expenditure of resources.

Remember, these are simply ways that Trump's tactics can be interpreted through the lens of Sun Tzu's principles. They do not necessarily mean that these tactics were intentionally derived from "The Art of War".

Final Reflection on the Art of Resilience

We can observe a profound embodiment of resilience in Dyson, Tesla, and Donald Trump. This quality transcends the ages of two thousand years ago from Sun Tzu's teaching in ancient China as it is in the challenges of the modern era.

Dyson's resilience is rooted in its persistent innovation and commitment to redefining what is possible within its market segment. Despite early failures and fierce competition, Dyson's relentless dedication to design and technological excellence demonstrates a profound resilience. Its ability to adapt, learn, and improve - drawing wisdom from its own experiences and the movements of its competitors - enables the company to maintain its leading position.

Under Elon Musk's vision and guidance, Tesla embodies resilience in the face of significant industry challenges and scepticism. While the auto industry was dominated by gas-powered vehicles, Tesla's unwavering commitment to electric cars defied conventional wisdom. The resilience of Tesla, like that of a true warrior, was reflected in its capacity to endure initial pushbacks, resist the status quo, and establish new norms, all while innovating at a pace that left competitors struggling to catch up.

Donald Trump, a divisive figure in modern politics, also demonstrates resilience. Despite widespread criticism and intense scrutiny, he ascended to the highest office in the U.S. and maintained a loyal support base. He navigates the complex landscape of politics, draws near to his audience, and rebounds from various controversies. Trump shows a form of resilience exemplified significantly by his political success.

In each of these examples - Dyson, Tesla, and Trump - we observe how the art of resilience manifests in the modern world. All faced adversity and challenges, yet their ability to endure, adapt, and push forward demonstrates a unique interpretation of Sun Tzu's wisdom in our modern context. The resilience they embody is not just about surviving the battles they face but about transforming these battles into foundations for success. It is an art as relevant in the boardrooms and marketplaces of today as it was on the battlefields of ancient China. Just as a single bamboo shoot can withstand the harshest storms, bending but not breaking, these modern examples show us that resilience - the ability to endure, adapt, and thrive amidst adversity - is timeless.

Afterword

Sun Tzu's teachings are more than a book about warfare; they encapsulate the essence of strategy, leadership, and management. Young and old readers may harness its wisdom across various facets of life, business, politics, sports, or everyday situations. The merit of this ancient text lies not just in its rich historical content but also in our ability to apply its principles to address contemporary issues and challenges.

"The Art of Resilience" aims to unlock the value of ancient Chinese teaching to today's practical uses. Comprehension is not merely a theoretical exercise; proper understanding is born from practical implementation. Whether capitalising on opportunities in a competitive business landscape or navigating life's daily struggles, practising "The Art of Resilience" empowers us to approach these situations differently.

Each of us is engaged in our own life's battles, facing challenges in our professional and personal lives. This book provides a unique framework for conceptualising and addressing these challenges.

In conclusion, I hope that your journey through "The Art of Resilience" equips you with a strategy tailored to your needs, aiding you in overcoming obstacles and achieving your goals. The road may be fraught with challenges, but success is within reach with perseverance.

As you finish reading "The Art of Resilience," may you gain a deeper understanding of Sun Tzu's wisdom, and may it guide you to success in your endeavours. Thank you for investing your time in this book, and I eagerly anticipate the triumphs that await you on your future journey.

About the Author:

Kenneth So has had a long and fruitful journey in global communication and publishing, stretching over forty years. He pioneered the launch of the International Business Journal in 1985, the first in English in China, and was supported by China's Ministry of Foreign Trade. This milestone showcased Kenneth as a forward-thinking publisher and editor in the field.

As the years rolled into the next decade, Kenneth widened his scope and brought popular lifestyle magazines "ELLE" and "Car & Driver" closer to Chinese readers through localised editions. This notable step opened the door to Western lifestyle insights in China. Kenneth also spearheaded the creative task of publishing in-flight magazines for Chinese airlines, offering enjoyable reads for travellers flying across China.

From 1995 to 2010, Kenneth's career branched out internationally as he became the Hong Kong Bureau Chief of Dempa Publications Inc. DPI, Japan's well-respected publishing house known for promoting the electronics industry since 1950. During this phase, Kenneth closely watched the evolving trends in electronics and technology across the Asia Pacific region.

Apart from publishing, Kenneth has a keen interest in practical philosophy. He is certified by APPA as a Philosophical Practitioner, which means he can provide counsel using philosophical principles to help people tackle life's problems. He's also a proud founding Hong Kong Practical Philosophy Society member.

Kenneth's extensive career experience and his love for practical philosophy have shaped him and provided a rich source of insights for handling the fast-paced changes of our modern world. His life's work highlights the beauty of innovation, cultural exchange, and in-depth analysis, also reflected in his book on Sun Tzu.

Printed in Great Britain
by Amazon